D1557360

THE ANGEL OF CHARLESTON

THE ANGEL OF CHARLESTON

Grace Higgens,
Housekeeper to the Bloomsbury Group

❦

STEWART MACKAY

THE BRITISH LIBRARY

To my wonderful parents, Kate and Duncan MacKay

First published in 2013 by

The British Library
96 Euston Road
London NW1 2DB

ISBN 978 0 7123 5867 5

Text © Stewart MacKay 2013

Extracts from the diaries of Grace Higgens
© The Estate of Grace Higgens 2013

Illustrations © The British Library Board
and other named copyright holders

Designed and typeset in Monotype Fournier by illuminati, Grosmont
Printed in Hong Kong by Great Wall Printing Co. Ltd

Contents

	ACKNOWLEDGEMENTS	vi
	Introduction	1
ONE	*Beginnings*	9
TWO	*Bloomsbury*	25
THREE	*South of France*	37
FOUR	*Style and Romance*	71
FIVE	*A Brave New World*	89
SIX	*Charleston*	101
SEVEN	*Legacies*	127
	Epilogue	139
	NOTES AND REFERENCES	145
	INDEX	150

Acknowledgements

T HERE ARE a great many people I should like to thank: my editor Lara Speicher for all her kindness, patience and constant support as well as Robert Davies for his astute advice; Wendy Hitchmough, Diana and the late John Higgens, Henrietta Garnett, Anne Olivier Bell, Simon Watney, Cressida Bell, Lindy Dufferin, Virginia Nicholson and, particularly, Richard Shone for all the many generous cups of tea, glasses of wine and suppers offered during my fascinating research. I would particularly like to extend my warmest thanks to John Higgens and his family, who have proved themselves so kind and generous during the research stages of this book. A kind and gentle man, John Higgens sadly passed away during the production of this book and I hope it may stand as a fitting memorial to his family's importance in the history of the Bloomsbury Group. Special thanks must also go to Henrietta Garnett for permission to quote from her grandmother, and to Pandora Smith and the Roche family for their kindness, wise advice and permission to quote from Clarissa Roche. It would without a doubt have been impossible to write this book without the inspirational Jamie Andrews and the curators of the British Library's Modern Literary Manuscripts department, as well as the staff and curators of the Tate Archive. To my greatest friends, who have been so forthcoming with unfailing encouragement, I offer my deepest gratitude.

Introduction

Charleston farmhouse today

We should ourselves be sorry to think that posterity should judge us by a patchwork of our letters, preserved by chance, independent of their context, written perhaps in a fit of despondency or irritation, divorced, above all, from the myriad little strands which colour and compose our peculiar existence, and which in their multiplicity, their variety and their triviality, are vivid to ourselves alone, uncommunicable even to those nearest to us, sharing our daily life.... Still, within our limitations it is necessary to arrive at some conclusions, certain facts do emerge.[1]

Vita Sackville-West

I T I S E A S Y for most people to believe they know the Bloomsbury Group inside out. The diaries and letters have been read, the novels written about, the paintings examined, the houses visited. By the end of the 1970s it seemed that in Britain many were experiencing a love affair with those early social and artistic pioneers. Their journey from early-twentieth-century radicalism to late-twentieth-century ubiquity is clearly indicative of Britain's unique ability to comfortably absorb a variety of cultural marginalia into the mainstream. It must not be forgotten, however, that the Bloomsberries, as the Group's members were sometimes called, were themselves already part of the Establishment – even if they didn't want to be: educated, independent, leisured, upper middle-class and, at least from a twenty-first-century perspective, complacent. Their class consciousness has, in recent decades, drawn a great deal of criticism, even if it was unexceptional for the period. There is an unresolved tension at the heart of 'Bloomsbury' which concerns an instinctive identification with, yet aesthetic repulsion from, the Establishment. Nevertheless they were full of optimism and hope in a utopian future, and to us, in the weary and sometimes cynical twenty-first century, an appreciation of Bloomsbury's social and artistic mission requires a certain suspension of disbelief, a generous act of empathy. The Bloomsbury Group's desire to reject many of the assumptions of the previous generation is one that anyone can identify with. It is never easy to escape the pressures of parental and social expectation about the shape one's life will take. It is because the members of Bloomsbury performed such a brave escape, and rewrote their personal histories – as well as for their creative and political output – that they are a grouping we can still admire today.

∽

In spite of the Bloomsbury Group's apparent ubiquity, few of us can have a complete picture of what it was really like to live among them. How fascinating it would be to have a truly fresh perspective upon life in Gordon Square or at Charleston farmhouse! Such a voice, which adds significantly to the Bloomsbury picture, has emerged from obscurity in recent years. Perhaps unsurprisingly this 'new' voice resoundingly echoes out from the heart of the house, 'below' the Turkish carpets and varnished floorboards. It is the voice of Grace Higgens, the Bloomsbury housekeeper described by Duncan Grant as the 'angel of Charleston', whose letters and diaries were acquired in 2007 by the British Library. As maid, nanny and later housekeeper in both London and Sussex, Grace spent fifty years in service to the Bloomsbury artists Vanessa Bell (1879–1961) and Duncan Grant (1885–1978). Vanessa's sister was the novelist Virginia Woolf (1882–1941), and Virginia's below-stairs Victorian 'leviathan'[2] becomes, in Grace, Vanessa Bell's very own modern yet motherly 'angel of the house'.

The irony is that – at least at Charleston – Grace was anything but 'below stairs', as she and her family lived very much at the top of the house, occupying the airy attic rooms beside Vanessa's studio. Grace wryly christened these quarters 'High Holborn', being as they were 'above Bloomsbury'. A further irony is that in the many photographs of her at Charleston as an older woman, the by then ailing Grace looks deeply proprietorial, a matron of the county afforded lifelong respect and admiration. According to her son John Higgens, her motto was 'always pay debts and compliments'. To those who knew her Grace was a lively, engaging and fashionably dressed woman held in fond regard.

⌒

Grace Higgens feels uncannily familiar and yet profoundly unknown; we already know so much about her famous employers, and yet her life has remained until now obscured. Reconstructing a personality from the 'scraps and fragments'[3] of a life is – as many Bloomsberries knew well enough – a complex business.

Aside from what Grace herself has written, little is known about her daily routines and travels between London and Sussex, though from the few diaries and letters she kept we can piece together a busy life spent amongst many of the great British figures of the twentieth century. For all the implicitly accepted class boundaries between Grace and Vanessa, and despite the strong socialist views espoused by Grace in her youth, these two formidable women lived affectionately together for fifty years. Grace remained in service until her retirement, and a mutual reverence grew between her and her employer. According to Vanessa's daughter-in-law Anne Olivier Bell, though Grace was 'a different class' and therefore beyond friendship, it must be acknowledged that she was treated with greater familial affection than most other domestic servants of her generation. Her relationship with the sometimes austere Vanessa and ever-friendly Duncan is examined here, as is her affectionate and somewhat unlikely friendship with the exotic Russian dancer Lydia Lopokova (1892–1981), wife of the economist John Maynard Keynes. Grace's diaries, particularly, give a unique glimpse into the everyday lives of the British avant-garde of the interwar period, as well as revealing her own opinions on politics, morality, class, travel, romance and domesticity.

The Grace Higgens Archive in the British Library contains several diaries (from 1921–22, 1924 and 1926), letters (mostly from the 1930s) and personal photographs. Much of Grace's writing is published here for the first time, along with many affectionate memories of those who knew her. I became fascinated by this little-known collection whilst working in the British Library's Manuscripts department in 2009–10. What struck me particularly was that it is one of the few personal collections held by the British

Library that belonged to a working-class woman: just the kind of person whose 'voice' would not have been thought important or valuable until comparatively recently. For this reason I approached the collection as well as the writing of this book with a real sense of privilege – as well as a smile, for it seems Grace was nothing if not a woman who enjoyed a giggle.

Always lucid and ever engaging, Grace's diaries possess a fluid and often idiosyncratic approach to spelling, punctuation and grammar. For ease and legibility I have taken the liberty of standardising some of the diary entries. Any mistakes in transcription are therefore entirely my own.

The lively and welcoming lynchpin of her Charleston world, Grace is described by writer Henrietta Garnett (a granddaughter of Vanessa Bell and Duncan Grant) as 'the backbone of Bloomsbury'.

Vanessa and Angelica Bell

ONE

Beginnings

Vanessa Bell

T HE DESIRE and the need for personal freedom permeated
the lives of Vanessa Bell and her friend (and one-time lover)
Duncan Grant; they steadfastly refused throughout their lives
to conform to convention. Although rather more conventional
than his free-thinking wife, Vanessa's husband, the critic Clive
Bell, appreciated her radicalism – as well as her lifelong desire
to avoid the conservative relations she was forced to humour in
her youth.

Gathered from the college lawns of Cambridge,[1] Vanessa and
Duncan's closest friends became their live-in family. Hierarch-
ical familial structures were consciously avoided in favour of
democratic, communal or, more specifically, collegiate living.
Clive came and went as he pleased. With Enlightenment and Romantic roots, the Cambridge philosopher G. E. Moore's *Principia
Ethica*, published in 1903, was an espousal of the positive value of
personal relations and the importance of personal freedom, and
it became the basis for the 'Bloomsbury philosophy': modern,
secular, inclusive, radical. Unable to reconcile such ideals with the

Duncan Grant with homemade turban

Clive Bell

social assumptions and conventions of the day – capitalism, imperialism, christianity, marriage, misogyny and so on – Vanessa, Duncan and their friends (already to some extent geographically marginal in their shabby London district of Bloomsbury) necessarily became 'outsiders': generally identifying as left-wing atheists because they refused to be subjugated by conservative and religious dogmas; branded bohemian because they valued a variety of sexual arrangements; passionate artists because they could afford to avoid the everyday tyranny of monotonous toil. Without negating the value of their liberal humanism, nowadays it can sound very much like a philosophy of the privileged few. One cannot forget the character Margaret Schlegel's admission in the Bloomsbury novelist E. M. Forster's *Howards End* (1910) that 'independent thoughts are in nine cases out of ten the result of independent means'.[2] Indeed, the capital upon which Vanessa and Clive's financial independence was based had been accumulated by ancestors of a decidedly more conservative hue, and consolidated out of investments made in the white heat of Victorian industrial and imperial expansion. And here is the defining Bloomsbury conflict: a desire for and a simultaneous rejection of the comfort and security of the previous generation.

Although Vanessa's family already knew Sussex well, the first to set up house there was her younger sister Virginia Stephen (later Woolf). In 1911, renting a small house in the then-isolated village of Firle, not far from the old town of Lewes, Virginia called it Little Talland House after her beloved childhood Talland House in Cornwall. A year later she and her sister were renting Asheham House just outside Beddington as a place to which they could escape from London. By 1916 Vanessa wanted to rent a Sussex house of her own, partly so that Duncan could join her there. As

Virginia and Leonard Woolf

conscientious objectors, he and his then-lover David 'Bunny' Garnett found work, initially in Norfolk, as farm labourers in order to avoid conscription or imprisonment. Vanessa's happening upon the modest farmhouse of Charleston (owned by Lord Gage of nearby Firle Park) meant that Duncan could move in and, for the rest of the war, work twelve-hour shifts for Mr Hecks the farmer at nearby New House Farm. Duncan, in fact, never left. Virginia remained at Asheham until 1919, when she and her husband Leonard[3] moved to Monk's House at Rodmell, not far from Charleston.

During the interwar period, spending time in Sussex became a calming salve to the sisters' sometimes complicated London lives. Surprisingly Charleston even provided more space to be creative than the high-ceilinged rooms of a London townhouse. Among the interwar English avant-garde there was a tendency for artistic engagement with the world to be negotiated in well-placed bourgeois seclusion. Requiring regular escapes from urban life, Vanessa and Duncan's was in many ways a very English modernism of retreat into a rural utopia, drawing inspiration from the nineteenth-century visions of William Morris, founder of the Arts and Crafts Movement.

E. M. ('Morgan') Forster loosely based the intellectual, bohemian (and independently wealthy) Schlegel sisters of *Howards End* on Vanessa and Virginia. Forster shows us that the Schlegels were always destined to 'inherit' Howards End and that the surrounding Hertfordshire countryside had been patiently waiting for their arrival. A hundred years later we might romantically imagine that Sussex, and specifically Charleston, was expectantly waiting to be Vanessa's home – destined to be found and claimed as utopian England. Today we cannot imagine Vanessa without Charleston or indeed Charleston without Vanessa. The house was never grand, and its shabbiness inspired stylistic improvements of an entirely modern hue. Its space, light, fresh air and dramatic downland views offered a place free of imposed constraints, allowing those who lived and stayed there to create a free-thinking enclave of defiant rural modernity. In their day this assortment of intellectuals and artists – to echo the academic Noel Annan – *was* the English avant-garde. The Bloomsbury Group's wide-ranging effects on British society are in many ways ubiquitous, as the critic Simon Watney has written: they 'pioneered and shaped many of the most important and attractive aspects of modern British life'.[4] Many of the social and artistic changes they pioneered were developed in the fertile intellectual hothouse of Charleston, and Grace Higgens was a key witness to those times.

Grace Jeanette Germany was born on 4 November 1903, the eldest of seven children of a farming family in Norfolk; her father George was a smallholder and, according to Vanessa's biographer Frances Spalding, who interviewed Grace in old age, her mother Elizabeth had once been maid to an obscure American artist called Sheldon Mills. Such a background may have equipped the young Grace not only with a constitution for hard work but also with an appreciation of the eccentricities of those with an artistic disposition. Her parents' farm, the main house of which was two cottages made into one, lay on a marshy fen about half a mile from the small village of Banham, itself about seven miles north of the town of Diss. Walking each day the two-mile rough track to the village school, Grace combined her studies with responsibilities (as eldest) in assisting her mother. The rearing of livestock, the growing of vegetables, the preparation of economical meals for

Grace as a young girl

large numbers of hungry mouths, the nurturing of small children: all were ideal training for her future career. But for a young girl of imagination and verve, an isolated farming life cannot have appeared satisfactory. In any case – as her son John Higgens believes – there wasn't enough paid work about, so the young Grace had little choice but to leave home.

In her own amusing and rather terse potted biography, written in the back of her 1921–22 diary, we learn that in 1917, aged only thirteen, she left her local school 'the week before Whitsun' and probably spent that summer and much of the following autumn working with her mother around the farm. But a different life, an independent life, and perhaps – for the adolescent Grace – the excitement and glamour of the capital beckoned. With the help of her parents, the fourteen-year-old Grace arranged that she should go, in the first week of December 1917, to live with her father's childless sister and her husband at suburban Hayes in Middlesex, just over ten miles from the centre of London. In the nineteenth century Hayes had become an industrial town providing factory work for vast numbers of skilled and unskilled labourers. Lodging with her aunt and uncle at 3 Priory Villas (since demolished), Grace immediately took a variety of jobs in 'stamp, jam and Gramophone factories'. However, Vanessa's granddaughter, the artist Cressida Bell, remembers Grace telling her about how she once worked in a chocolate factory and how all the free chocolate put her off such creamy delicacies for life. Perhaps this was just a good yarn for the children.

On 20 December 1917, in her own words, Grace was 'wired home by father' for her mother was 'lying seriously ill with pneumonia and expected to die'. Immediately returning to Banham, she nursed her mother back to health and stayed to take over her mother's household duties until the beginning of spring 1918. By 1 May she was told her aunt was planning a visit and would take her back to Priory Villas upon her return. Perhaps Grace did not enjoy living with her middle-aged aunt and uncle, for, despite giving no reason even in her diary, she 'begged mother and father' to allow her to go instead into domestic service. Though he cannot be sure, Grace's son John believes her that uncle-in-law may have proved himself inappropriately affectionate.

Whatever the truth of the situation, Grace was evidently dissatisfied at Hayes and perhaps frustrated at Banham – so much so that, once permitted, she happily applied for domestic positions which required not only a drop in pay but also restrictions upon her free time. 'As a general societal trend, after the First World War, … younger girls regarded service as an occupation of last resort. Many moved from job to job very frequently, in search of better conditions.'[5] This was perhaps less so for young women such as Grace who came from backgrounds of rural poverty. Without paid work on the family farm there was now no other choice for Grace but domestic service. Father and mother at first protested but finally gave in and wrote for a place that had been advertised in the *Daily Express* with Dr Sprowart of St Stephen House, Newmarket Road, Norwich. Off to Norwich she went, capable though inexperienced. According to Grace, Dr Sprowart was not an easy man to work for. She 'was very unhappy with the Doctor; [he] had an awful temper'. For nearly two years Grace accepted her situation, until she

> left on May the Eighth 1920. Stayed at home with mother and father for a month; then applied for housemaids place at Collins agency, Prince of Wales Road, Norwich. From there got Mrs Bell's address and so came to London on the 30th June 1920.

The social historian Pamela Horn has recently asserted that country girls were 'used to firm discipline at home and regularly helped with domestic chores' and would therefore, when in service, 'accept their lot without a fuss'.[6] Unlike Grace, young women brought up in large towns and cities had more options for work – usually in hotels or factories – which had the advantage of more sociable hours, better working conditions and better pay. It was in these circumstances that *The Times* began publishing obituaries extolling the virtues of 'Faithful Servants' who had remained with the same family for many decades.[7] After the First World War, middle-class employers of servants began to notice a wane in the supply of cheap, undemanding labour. Many of the young women who would previously have jumped at the chance of domestic employment knew that working life could be better elsewhere, in hotels, factories, shops or, if they were lucky, in an office. The hardships of war had naturally changed working-class expectations. Middle-class employers realised that if they still wanted domestic servants they would have to modify their own expectations, and make some serious concessions. The ease with which servants could move to other jobs was a feature of the interwar servant scarcity, and it helped to encourage mistresses to improve working conditions so as to retain their staff.[8] It is astonishing to consider that, according to her daughter-in-law Diana Higgens, Grace never once asked for a raise in her salary during the entire fifty years she spent with the Bells. Yet Pamela Horn has drawn attention to research undertaken in 1937 that reveals that, reasonably, 'pay was not a major grievance, when compared to the issues of working hours and leisure opportunities'.[9]

Grace had a respectable level of experience as a housemaid in Norwich (not least in coping with a volatile employer), a hard-working rural background and a perky disposition, and at sixteen was still young enough to be considered malleable; and Vanessa happily accepted her services. Correspondence between Vanessa and Duncan reveals frequent nervous tension concerning inadequate servants at Charleston during and just after the First World War, so it came as a significant relief to discover Grace and her steady domestic grip – especially as she arrived just after housemaid Mary sadly lost her mind (bizarrely, only after *pretending* she had lost her mind following a series of concocted family disasters and impersonations that sent Vanessa on a wild-goose-chase around Bedfordshire in the hope of establishing the truth).[10] It was Mary's eventual certification as mentally unstable that necessitated her replacement.

In spite of her youth, Grace must have appeared stability itself after poor Mary. She was hired a month after being interviewed by Vanessa in London, initially as nursemaid to Vanessa's children: twelve-year-old Julian, nine-year-old Quentin and particularly the one-year-old Angelica Bell (Duncan Grant's natural daughter).[11] Grace 'went to Charleston with Mrs Bell on 30 July [1920]'. Fifty years later she firmly asserted in a recorded interview with Quentin Bell that she arrived at Charleston on Vanessa's birthday, 30 May.[12] She stayed at Charleston for a time, learning the ropes, before returning to London with Vanessa in mid-October 1920 to settle for the winter at Gordon Square. In this first year with the Bells, living and working between London and Sussex, she was given a month at home in Norfolk for Christmas and more than a week off during the following summer. On her return to the Bell household after the latter break, Grace writes in her diary, 'I got a letter from Mum, they are looking forward to seeing me soon. I expect they will then look forward to see me come away. But I hope they will not.'

With varied work, changing scenery, gossiping colleagues, interesting employers and long holidays, being a housemaid for the Bells must have felt a good deal more exciting than monotonous factory work at Hayes. Although Grace may sometimes have appeared young and flighty, her Norfolk accent was considered 'calming' and reassuring: no mean attribute for a lifelong domestic career. Years later, when considering the pivotal role occupied by Grace, 'Bunny' Garnett would write to Duncan's young friend, the writer Richard Shone, 'then by the Grace of God came Grace'. Richard Shone remembers even Grace's footsteps to be calming – naturally light and unobtrusive. The writer Henrietta Garnett (daughter of 'Bunny' Garnett and Angelica Bell) asserts that the family 'didn't believe in God – but they did believe in Grace'.

To the general reader, the only mention of Grace – until now – was found fleetingly in Frances Spalding's masterful biographies of Vanessa and Duncan, and yet even these cursory glimpses demonstrate her influence on the household. Spalding asserts the Bell family's view that Grace could adapt to any situation and turn her hand to almost anything. Vanessa's son, the art historian Quentin Bell, recalls in his foreword to Diana Higgens's privately printed collection of memoirs and recipes, *Grace at Charleston*, that when Grace arrived in the employ of his mother, she was a lively, innocent, forgetful and easily startled girl, coping in the most amiable manner with the eccentricities and vagaries of artists and their friends.[13] And Spalding goes on to say, 'She adapted willingly to any task – parlour maid, nurse, cook, housekeeper – becoming more and more invaluable ... But wherever she found herself, Grace was amused and interested in the life which went on around her.'[14] Grace's charm could be immense, possessed as she was of an essentially joyful outlook on the world. The security and routine of domestic life, and the respect afforded her by her employers, only served to strengthen her contentment.

An entry from her 1924 diary reveals a young woman bursting with joy: 'I do not worry & I always feel so happy I could love everybody.' Such an attitude must surely explain her lasting success at Charleston.

TWO

Bloomsbury

C ONSIDERED by high society for much of the early twentieth century to be definitely 'out', Bloomsbury was a charming though shabby district on the outer fringes of London gentility. On and off it was home to Vanessa for most of her life. Eschewing any conventional regularity, she, Clive, Virginia, Duncan and their friends moved between Bloomsbury and various rented weekend or holiday houses mostly as and when they pleased – the motivation often a desire to paint or write in quiet. The district of Bloomsbury was, for Vanessa and Duncan, far enough away (physically and psychologically) from their rather conventional familial circles to make it instantly desirable. Its relative affordability and proximity to the intellectual and non-conformist havens of the British Museum, University College and the Slade School of Art made it even more attractive for those in pursuit of personal and artistic freedom.

Grace, though, could hardly have registered the minutiae of such middle-class concerns, and Bloomsbury must have presented itself to her simply as London: an enormous novelty, hard to categorise. For Vanessa, with her private means, personal freedom was more easily attained; and having domestic servants meant that the mundanity of daily life could sometimes be conveniently avoided. She could afford a London home, a country home and, years later, a holiday home in the Mediterranean sun. But in order to be free to paint she had to be confident that her homes were clean, the children were being properly looked after, food was ordered and prepared on time, the garden in Sussex was productive and so forth. Vanessa needed domestic stability, and Grace became her right-hand woman.

For much of the interwar period Charleston possessed no gas, electricity or indeed running water, but life there was not overly arduous: in the employ of Vanessa, Clive and Duncan, Grace and her fellow domestics appear to have enjoyed a comparatively relaxed working atmosphere. When the Bell household was resident in London, Grace's evenings were often spent at the local cinemas or theatres and, although Grace was not a drinker, during the summers in Sussex, evening trips to the local pub were frequent. Grace was lucky in her employers. Vanessa was financially comfortable enough to employ three or four below-stairs staff as well as a gardener and various odd-job men, most of whom would move with the family between London and Sussex as her life and work dictated. This meant that at least during the interwar years Grace was never a 'maid of all work'. Grace's life was very different from that of her mother when she had been a parlour maid in the Victorian age; life had changed and newer freedoms were afforded. Pay increased slightly and, as a general national trend, modern technology meant that less laborious work was expected of most servants. For Grace, however, it was only after the Second World War – when she was solely in charge of domestic life at Charleston – that modern appliances were bought in the hope of easing her daily burden.

Grace wrote diaries seriously, with intent and energy, only during a five-year period in the early to mid-1920s. This was the time in her life when she had the time to write a diary and the youthful inclination to do so, as well as the need for a private outlet to express her feelings, living as she was in such close proximity to fellow servants. Given the paucity of surviving diaries, piecing together Grace's life, as a life set apart from her famous employers, is a challenge, and her generally deferential attitude to them is hard to comprehend today, though it was typical of employer–servant relationships during the period. A genuine delight in dressing up and being silly endeared Grace to the Bloomsberries – but they, her employers, were of course different from most other people. In the early days her diary demonstrates a very adolescent self-consciousness about being set apart:

> In the afternoon Quentin & I took the Gramophone to be mended. We did look freaks prancing along. Quentin with green socks falling over his shoe tops and me with a huge Gramophone very badly done up, tucked under one arm & my frock all hitched on one side.

Being an adjunct to an 'odd' family took some getting used to, and might even prove dangerous. Walking the streets of London, five-year-old Angelica

> persisted in holding my hand very tightly & singing at the top of her voice that the soldier was running away, so intent was I in listening to her that I nearly got run over by an errand boy on a bicycle affair.

After a morning's work, Grace often (at least in London) enjoyed time off in the afternoons. She would go walking, shopping or attend the new cinemas; 'oh it's good to be alive'. According to her son John, Grace remembered having, on one particular trip to the theatre, a sneezing fit behind King George V, an involuntary act the memory of which always made her giggle as the years passed. Everything was new and strange in the capital. She recounted seeing 'a rather large black monkey' sitting in the window of a shop in the Tottenham Court Road

> making frantic efforts to get out of a cage. The poor creature would get one bar at [a] time and shake with all its might. I was awfully sorry for it, I think it is wicked to keep these poor creatures shut up in beastly little iron cages.

She found London bizarre and fascinating:

> It is worthwhile to stand in a [shopping] queue if it is only to see that strange medley of street performers, who gather round to collect money and dance, sing, act & play every kind of musical instrument.

London had the delights of shopping and the glamour of the cinema, but the romantic Grace noticed and enjoyed the quiet simple things too:

> The air smells of violets. I expect it is too early for them but still it smells of them.
> It was very nice this morning, the air was lovely & smelly, it makes your nose keep twitching like a dogs to smell it; it is so good.

The city buzzed and hummed to the beat of multicultural modern life. Out with her younger sister Alice, down from Norfolk for a holiday, Grace records:

> We had coffee in an Italian shop in Tottenham Court Road ...
> they served the coffee in very weird glasses in silver stands with
> a big spoon like a soup ladle.

Yet the streets of London to the country girl proved unnecessarily
expensive.

> We had ices in the Tottenham Court Road & saw the weirdest
> little dog which managed to escape from its lead ... it cost 25
> pounds – I would rather have had the money.

Mostly Grace relished her time in the city, and although it seemed
to rain fairly often, she imagined the streets as thrilling caverns
of endless romance.

> There was a man singing outdoors tonight, I could love him.
> He had a lovely voice all quivery & a mandolin. He sang in
> Italian a sweet pathetic song & then he sang 'Pale Hands of
> Love' from the Indian Love Lyrics, in very bad English.

In establishing her voice, Grace often wrote about the weather,
using it initially as a prompt to describe her feelings and then
as a springboard to an examination of deeper issues. Such a
technique is sometimes vivid and extremely sensuous, evoking
lines from a Woolf novel or juxtapositions in a Bell painting.
Awakening to a sunny sky could sometimes produce a curiously
melancholic effect:

> It was a lovely morning, the kind that shows up all the cobwebs
> and dust & the marks on your last year's costume.

Sometimes, though, life temporarily got muddled:

> A dreadful thing happened. Mrs Bell came & called me this
> morning instead of me calling her.

Listening to crowds singing on the wireless she wrote that 'it was most beautiful, like heaven opened & you could hear the angels singing'. This sensitivity to beauty was one of several similarities between Grace and her mistress. Unlike Virginia Woolf and her maid Nellie Boxall, there was no deep-rooted psychological struggle between Vanessa and Grace. Sadly, like any family with three children living in London, the Bells could not avoid the relatively new dangers of a modern metropolis:

> Such a beastly day. Angelica and Louie¹ were run over by a motorcar. Louie has been brought home, Angelica is in Middlesex hospital. ... Everyone very upset ... A lovely day but everyone miserable. ... Mrs Bell has been in tears for most part of the day. Mrs Bell, Mr Grant & Mr Bell had their blood tested in case an operation is needed on Angelica. ... Angelica very cheerful. ... Louie hops about. ... Patients getting on as well as can be expected.

Unlike many employers of the day, the Bells were generous to Grace and did not avoid encouraging her intellectual development.

> Mr [Clive] Bell, Julian & Quentin arrived about tea time. They brought me lots of books.

According to diary entries, in April 1922 Grace was enthusiastically reading Jonathan Swift's *Gulliver's Travels* and by the end of August 1924 had finished reading J. J. Morier's exotic *Hajji Baba* adventures. With characteristic modesty Grace claimed she could not read Virginia Woolf's novels: 'I just couldn't get interested in them. Perhaps I wasn't intelligent enough.'² Yet from the South of France in 1927, Vanessa reported to Clive that Grace was reading Nikolai Gogol's *Dead Souls*. Duncan's friend Richard Shone believes Grace read Sigmund Freud's *The Interpretation of Dreams*, which is not far-fetched given that its English translation was undertaken by Lytton Strachey's younger brother James (someone she must have met on several occasions) and that the Woolfs' Hogarth Press published Freud's collected papers. A story that Duncan apparently liked to tell, and relayed to me by Richard Shone, concerns the painter and set designer Robert Medley, who in 1929 stopped Vanessa in London's Fitzroy Street to discover her views on D. H. Lawrence's privately published novel *Lady Chatterley's Lover*. Vanessa is said to have replied that, as she had of course only one copy, she'd have to let him know – because 'Grace is reading it'. If the story is true, Vanessa's liberalism is significant. Even thirty years later during the novel's obscenity trial, the chief prosecutor famously questioned whether it was the sort of book one would wish the servants to read. It seems that Vanessa had no such qualms.

One of the Bells' temporary housemates at Gordon Square was the Russian dancer Lydia Lopokova[3], known as 'Loppy', who was soon to become the wife of the Bloomsbury economist John Maynard Keynes. Free of English class prejudice, Lydia would happily sit in the kitchen with Grace drinking tea and gossiping – and perhaps recommending the works of Gogol. It must have been heartening to relax in this way, as much for Lydia as for Grace. Both probably understood the dispiriting effects of British class snobbery, and the inner sanctum of Bloomsbury somewhat condescended to Lydia, whose ambitious father had been an usher at the Alexandrinsky Theatre in St Petersburg. Many underestimated her charm, beauty and intellect, but Grace never did. Frances Spalding has written how Grace 'listened with delight' as Lydia entertained her with 'tales of Old Russia, of samovars, *droshkis* and boyars.[4] Both women were, in very different ways of course,

Lydia and John Maynard Keynes

Bloomsbury 'intimates' as well as distinct outsiders. In April 1922 Grace notes how often Lydia is 'in' for lunch, tea or supper; one day she 'gave me a basket … with Easter Eggs' and another day 'some gorgeous coloured pyjamas' (a mixed gift, for Grace had to borrow two pounds to repay Lydia). Lydia's evident talents and glamorously obscure foreignness provided an easy entry to high society, but she may have identified with Grace, seeing in her a vision of her own life, had she not been lucky enough to escape Communist Russia. One day Lydia even kindly 'gave me 3s [shillings] to buy jewellery with'. Such a friendship – perhaps Grace's first Bloomsbury 'friendship' – was a transgressive one. She often writes, for example, that she'd thrillingly gone with the boys to see Loppy dance. She regularly experienced the thrill of reading about her friend in the London gossip columns:

> I saw in the Daily Mirror that Madame Lydia Lopokova is suing her husband for a divorce on the grounds that his first marriage had not been properly dissolved when he married her. I suppose when she gets her divorce Mr [Maynard] Keynes will marry her. At present she is dancing at the London Coliseum & has given Quentin & I tickets for Saturday.

Maynard married 'Loppy' the following year. According to Richard Shone she could always make Grace laugh. Whilst later living with Maynard at Tilton, just down the road from Charleston, Loppy would often drop in to see Grace. Kitchen-table chatter and gossip became part of their respective Sussex routine, right up until Loppy's death in 1981 at a Seaford nursing home, only two years before Grace's own death.

The most striking aspect of Grace's diaries is their humour. It is not an obvious humour and she apparently does not seek to be funny. But there is a continuous streak of the absurd that runs through the diaries, so much so that almost every entry reads with a smile. Like many young people Grace sometimes enjoyed laughing at older people – at 'poor Mrs Upp',[5] for example, spied through the net curtains as she carefully negotiated the snow and the ice on her way to work one cold February morning. Grace's writing is often blunt, as when she and Quentin visit the fair: we 'spent some money & got nothing in return'. With her lively but dreamy young mind elsewhere she was often clumsy: 'I had a mishap, I fell up the stairs with a tray & broke one of the Spanish sugar basins, besides other sundry things.' And according to Julian, writing from Cassis in 1928, Grace 'mistook a bottle of brandy for water and drank a tumblerful'[6] – quite a feat for a woman who never enjoyed drinking. Nevertheless Grace is remembered to have often remarked how 'I've a naughty sense of humour', and in this she no doubt found a kindred spirit in Duncan. Most charmingly of all, she had a sometimes disarming habit of letting out a great scream of laughter and slapping the back or shoulder of whomever was nearest. It is remembered as one of her distinguishing characteristics.

Listening to recordings of Grace and her colleagues, we can compare accents. Grace's accent is rather different from those of Virginia Woolf's servants Nellie Boxall, Lottie Hope and Louie Mayer. Certainly as an older lady at least, Grace's voice was decidedly light and girlish – more controlled, without 'vulgar' outburst, and a little more refined, with far fewer flat vowels. Only occasionally does she reveal the warm undercurrents of the East Anglian accent everybody who knew her fondly remembers. Naturally her accent would change – partly due to her 'self-improvement' and partly to the new inter/postwar physical proximity she and other domestic servants now had with their tremulously voiced employers. Again, Virginia Woolf famously observed – not without a trace of discomfort – that by the 1920s modern servants were in and out of the drawing room asking to read the papers. By that time, at least for the Bloomsberries, servants were valued enough to be sitters and subjects of paintings, a tradition carried through from Vanessa's great-aunt, the pioneering early photographer Julia Margaret Cameron (1815–1879), who photographed her own maid. In both cases the lady of the house renders her charge safely picturesque. Vanessa's portrait of Grace in *The Kitchen* looks scarcely like the Grace we see in surviving photographs. The relationship between artist and sitter has great potential for intimacy, but, as was convention at the time, neither Vanessa nor Grace knew – nor expected to know – each other well enough for a mutual closeness to flourish. Affection, perhaps, but not intimacy. In an interview with Quentin Bell recorded in 1969 and conducted in the kitchen at Charleston as she busied herself in the preparation of a pudding, Grace remembers the times she was asked to sit for Vanessa and Duncan ('I'm afraid I'm a bad sitter') and, without any sense of disappointment, she believes that her portraits from the South of France have 'been lost'. Regarding her portrait by Duncan, sat for in the studio at Charleston during the late 1960s, with characteristic modesty she claims, 'I look rather fierce; I'm not using my glasses.' Yet Richard Shone remembers Duncan exclaiming, 'without her spectacles, she really is *very* handsome!'

THREE

South of France

Julian and Clive Bell at Cassis

G RACE's first visit abroad was to St Tropez during the winter of 1921–22, with Vanessa, Duncan, the children (thirteen-year-old Julian, eleven-year-old Quentin, and Duncan's natural daughter, three-year-old Angelica Bell) and their nanny Nellie Brittain. With Vanessa and her husband Clive enjoying a relatively unconventional marriage as independent individuals, Clive chose to spend the winter at home in England. Though there were to be several family trips to the South of France over the years it was Grace's first which was, according to her son John, her most memorable. Leaving London on 8 October 1921 and arriving at what was then the small seaside village of St Tropez on 11 October, the sights, sounds, smells and vivid 'otherness' of France made a lasting impression on the naïve seventeen-year-old.

The journey was an arduous, sometimes confusing and chaotic one, but it had a certain thrill about it. Outside of England and its usual social confines, travelling *en masse* in foreign parts created a feeling of communality amongst the group and produced a slight relaxation of conventions between maidservant and mistress. Vanessa mentions in letters held by the Tate Archive how Grace and the children all fell asleep in her lap on the train. Yet one can imagine both Grace and even the well-travelled Vanessa trying deliberately to cultivate a self-conscious sophistication whilst abroad, unable to quite shake off a very English desire to appear unperturbed by the heat and the dust.

> When we arrived at St Raphael we were quite unprepared & had to rush very quickly to get our luggage out (which we threw through the window) before the train started again. Mr [Roger] Fry¹ was waiting on the platform; he had come to meet us from St Tropez. Then as we all had 25 minutes to wait, we all trooped off to one of those dear little outdoor Cafés (which you never see in England, but which are so common in France) to have Coffee.

The train from Paris – possibly the famed 'Blue Train' designed specifically to transport visitors to the South – had been, Grace writes, 'smart inside', although the connecting trains from St Raphael were rather more basic. After changing trains once more, things got worse:

> I had thought the last train bad enough, but when I saw the one standing in the station & which we had to go in, I thought I should never recover, for I am sure cattle trucks in England look far cleaner than the carriage into which we got.

The seats were covered in a green material, but were

> all torn, and thick with dirt & dust. I tried to brush a little of the dust off & nearly got smothered so gave it up as a bad job & looked [out] of the windows, two of which had their glasses knocked out.

Roger Fry

Finally arriving in the little station at St Tropez, they were met by 'an interested little crowd of men and children' who 'collected to stare at us'. Freed of their luggage, which they left on the platform for the porters to send on to La Maison Blanche, their rented house just outside the village,

> Mrs Bell & Mr Fry went to buy some pastries, Mr Grant, Julian, Quentin, Nellie & myself sat down at a table in one of the cafes, where it said on a notice 'English spoken here' and watched the harbour. After tea we walked to La Maison Blanche.

Grace's initial impressions of St Tropez were not favourable:

> I was very glad we were not living in the town, as I never smelled anything that smelled so abominably as the French houses and streets; for the people seem to empty all their refuse into the streets and do not seem to mind in the least the disgusting smells, for they collect in numbers of five or six and sit and gossip and knit nearly all day long. I don't know when they do their work.

Arriving at the house, understandably exhausted, they were thrilled to find that the 'person who lived in the Lodge [Madame Santucci] had been kind enough to get us some supper ready' so they happily sat down to eat, and after making up 'sufficient beds' retired 'as soon as possible'.

When they awoke to a blue Mediterranean sky the following morning, the arrangement of rooms needed attention.

> I got one of the nicest rooms, Nellie & Angelica slept in the one facing the sea, on the same landing as myself; also there is a dear little dressing room which we share between us. Mrs Bell slept in the room above, Mr Grant & Julian below.

The house seemed to suit, its position truly idyllic:

> La Maison Blanche is a very nice house situated nearly on top
> of a hill overlooking the sea; looking from the windows the
> scenery was lovely, as far away you could see mountains, below
> which lay the sea which looked a beautiful deep blue, then just
> below us was St Tropez with its white houses and coloured
> shutters which you very rarely saw open. At the back of the
> house were hills all covered with pine woods and vine woods
> which looked very nearly as lovely as the front and side views.

Lunch was taken outside – quite a novelty for Brits in October
– and then the whole party decamped to the beach for the dreaded
revelation of white English flesh, where they were later met by
Roger Fry.

> It was quite a long distance, and the roads cover your ankles
> with dust so we were very tired when we arrived. We found it
> to be a very quiet place and had to pass through a small Café
> to get there, so it suited us very well as I for one do not like
> a crowd, as I cannot swim much and feel very self-conscious
> when anybody is looking at me. Neither Nellie or I went in the
> sea as we had not taken our bathing costumes, but Julian &
> Quentin had a dip.

After tea at the beach café, Vanessa and Duncan went to Roger's
for dinner, and Grace and Nellie accompanied Angelica and the
boys home for an early night's rest.

Grace's first early start began the following day:

> I got up at seven o'clock & lit the kitchen fire as La Bon
> [Louise, the local French 'daily'] did not arrive until 8.30am
> which was after breakfast which we had at eight o'clock. We
> had breakfast outside then I did usual work.

Initially, Louise did not make a favourable impression upon Grace
but quickly she realised what a great help she would prove.

Well, the first morning I came down and saw her I thought I should not like her. She is a typical little Frenchwoman and stands about five feet high, has dark hair, dark eyes and round face, which is lined as if she has had anxieties. She was married about eight months ago, but I have come to the conclusion that she does not like married life and wishes she were single. My opinion has altered … and Louise (that is her name) and I get on very well together. She has taught me quite a lot of French, which I find very useful.

Even Vanessa noticed Grace's improving French. After lunch she and Nellie got the children ready for an afternoon at the beach, packing swimming costumes and the vital post-swim food supplies. This was to prove a momentous day for Grace for not only did she slip into a bathing costume, she also swam for the first time.

I had never been in the sea before and I thought swimming must be very easy as I watched Julian and Quentin, so I dashed into the water and promptly fell over backwards. I thought I was going to be drowned, I could not get up, I tried to shout, but only got my mouth full of salt water. I had sunk twice and was just going down for the third time when Nellie managed to grab me. She could not swim any more than I and I nearly dragged her under, but she had a firm hold on the diving board. I had had enough of swimming to last me for the afternoon and nothing could get me to let go of the diving board, till I was near enough to the beach, so the water barely covered my ankles. After we had dressed we had tea on the beach, after which Mr Fry and Mr Grant came down with Mrs Bell and had a dip.

This was not to be her last swim, for there are accounts from Vanessa that on a trip to Cassis in 1928 Grace was plunging into the sea again.

Life at La Maison Blanche quickly settled into a routine somewhere between that of Gordon Square and that of Charleston. In the mornings Grace was put to work: there were beds to be made, carpets to be aired, dusting, brushing and mopping to be done, laundry to be scrubbed and food to be prepared. But – unless Angelica was unsettled ('Angelica does nothing but cry all day long') – in the afternoons there was fun to be had with Nellie. The boys spent their mornings in lessons with Mademoiselle Bouvet in St Tropez. Julian, as the eldest, felt a constant need for adventure and would often cajole Grace, against her better judgement, into accompanying him on his afternoon excursions. Grace had a sisterly attitude to the Bell children, who were relatively close to her own age, and in accordance with an old luck-bringing tradition Grace 'remembered to say "Rabbits Rabbits" this morning' before saying anything else. On the occasion of adventures though, like the characters from an Edwardian children's novel, they always arrive home crucially 'in time for tea'.

> After lunch, as I had promised Julian that I would go with him, we went exploring; we went through some vine-yards up a hill, through a pine-wood, where I scratched my legs and arms severely with brambles and got bitten with mosquitoes, so that when I emerged at the top of the hill I was feeling very sore; also very bad tempered Julian having lost his hat a good many times was not feeling much better. We decided on following a road which looked as if it led to the sea. So we walked down that wretched road for about two miles and we were both feeling fit to drop and the sea looked just as far away as it did in the beginning, so we sat down on a big bundle of cork and had a rest. Then we started our weary homeward journey. We arrived back in time for tea. I had had enough of exploring.

Simple walks could prove interesting and unusual:

> Went for a walk to the beach with Julian, Nellie and Angelica
> searching for shells. We were not very successful but got a few
> of the Periwinkle variety. When going down, an enormous
> insect flew into my dress, very much like a Praying Mantis in
> the shape of its body; but instead of green it was brown. Julian
> was very disappointed he had not his poison pot, not having got
> one of that species.

By early November Grace, Nellie and the children were following
local custom by going out each afternoon gathering fir-cones to
burn on the fire in the evenings; this continued regularly until
they departed for England in January. They often brought home
impressive hauls.

Grace was always game for fun and irreverence:

> Afterwards Julian, Quentin and I went to see two ruined
> Pillars on top of a hill and scratched our initials on them with a
> penknife. Came back for tea.

Sometimes, though, youth did not favour Grace, especially when
being told off:

> I am possessed of a very red nose, to the great amusement of
> La Bon [Louise]. Julian and I went on a fir-cone hunt, got a
> very respectable heap which we hid in a hollow when a virago
> [a bad-tempered woman] came with her family and ordered
> us off and bagged the lot. Arrived home for tea, feeling very
> ill-treated.

But she did know where to draw the line and when to discipline
the children:

> Went for a walk with Nellie to St Tropez, to do some shopping,
> Julian came and on the way insulted Nellie who therefore gave
> him a bit of her mind. Julian apologised and looked very small.

Angelica Bell and Judith Bagenal,
daughter of Vanessa's friend the artist Barbara Bagenal,
in the South of France

I afterwards went sticking with Julian, Nellie not coming as it rained.

That evening 'both Nellie and myself very indignant all evening about something told us'. Grace's diary does not record exactly what was said or indeed who said it – we can only guess. But Julian's adolescent appetite often dominated the day's routine:

Went for picnic after lunch. Julian insisted upon having tea at 3pm, after collecting a good supply of chips and fir-cones, came home about 4pm and had another tea.

On 28 November:

After Lunch, Mrs Bell and Mr Grant went painting and Julian and myself went to get some fir cones in the big forest on the hills. Julian and I got lost and could not find our way out. Julian deserted me and left me to find my way out. Following a track I at last reached the outskirts and saw Mrs Bell and Mr Grant painting. Julian had arrived first. We got a good supply of fir-cones and were all coming home together when Julian argued so much we had to part company [with Bell and Fry], he and I coming home by the vine-yards … We had tea very late, never went out after.

On 2 December, as though accompanying pestering younger brothers, 'Julian, Quentin and myself went shopping in St Tropez; they bought two pistols [and] afterward practised them on me.' Then a few days later 'Quentin bought some fireworks and let them off on the stove.' Whilst the story might appear funny to us, the boys' mischievousness must sometimes have been tiresome to Grace. A classic case occurred on 7 December:

I had to remain in my room all the afternoon, as the boys would not let me out until I told them the name and described my young man in St Tropez. Mrs Bell eventually rescued me.

Towards the end of October, Grace and Nellie were venturing into St Tropez itself. But running errands in the South of France was not quite like running errands along the Tottenham Court Road, and their trips 'into town' were more often than not guided by the demands of the children:

> After lunch, Nellie and I thought we would do some shopping [as] Mrs Bell wanted me to get a hat and some shoes for Quentin. We left the principle of the shopping to do when we came back and went down to the beach and had tea. Coming back I bought the hat after some difficulty as the shopman had not one large enough. Quentin wanted to buy some nougat and took us to a new place where I had not been before.

On their early trips into St Tropez Grace encountered ordinary French people on a daily basis for the first time: pale, and evidently self-conscious, 'we incited some curiosity in the inhabitants of the street as to who we were; as they came and stared and jabbered in French.'

23 October was set for the household's first day trip to a 'little bay three miles away'. They got up early:

> We were ready to start about nine thirty with our food all packed up and nearly everything ready. It was a long and wearisome journey and very difficult at times to drag the push chair wherein rode little Angelica, so we were very glad when we arrived.
>
> It was a lovely sight, the sand was silvery white and at first reminded one of powdered snow, the sea a beautiful deep blue. After we had had a rest we all except Mrs Bell changed into our bathing costumes and went for a dip. After which Nellie and I going into a little hut to dress turned Mr Grant out, the poor man having left his trousers inside, had to trot about with his shirt safety-pinned between his legs to prevent it blowing up.

When we were dressed we all went to a pine-wood nearby and had luncheon, which we all enjoyed very much. With luncheon over, Nellie, Julian, Quentin and myself went searching for shells. We got a very good variety of very pretty ones. The sand near the sea seems composed nearly of tiny little shells and pieces, which must have taken centuries to collect together.

The little boys then had another dip; after which we all had tea, then started home. The homeward journey was much harder than the going, as it was very windy and clouds of dust blew into our faces all the way. When at last we reached home we were all very tired but had enjoyed ourselves very much.

Their day trip was well planned as it turned out, as the following day brought with it wind and rain, rough seas and salt-spray. Vanessa, Duncan and Roger – along with several local or visiting friends – occupied themselves reading and painting together and dining both in and out. But as ever the boys were eager to escape the confines of the house, so Grace took them shopping, along the pier and 'we went up to the lighthouse, coming back to tea'. This sudden turn in the weather lasted several days, and brought more cold air and lashing rain ('the wind is very strong and the shutters and doors are continually creaking'). Such familiar weather made Grace miserable, so that she developed 'a very bad cold and sore throat' and felt 'very home-sick'. She 'longed for Old England and Home' and a day later she had resolved to mitigate her feelings by writing 'a long letter to Mum and Dad, then perhaps I shall feel better'.

Mercifully, a few days later 'the wind has dropped ... and it is quite warm', bringing to La Maison Blanche a more cheerful atmosphere. The following day too 'I felt much better as I received a letter from Mum and my cold is better'.

I had a very rude awakening this morning. I woke up to hear
someone hammering on the front door; throwing on my coat
I hurried down and found the milkmaid very wrathful. I had
forgotten the milk can, one of the instances in which I found it
to my advantage not to understand French. I went shopping in
the afternoon then went to Mr Fry's lodgings. It is a rather nice
little house facing a bay where there is a big collection of cuttle
fish bones. Afterwards going round the town, then home.

By the end of October 1921 everyone had established a permanent
routine and they began to settle down for the winter. Grace
regularly called French civic pride into question, sounding rather
like a stereotypical suburban English lady; already she was

> getting fed up with marching through the town as the streets
> smell disgusting and there are no shops worth going to see, so
> we are for the future going to try the opposite direction. But it
> has not much attraction as the roads are beastly.

And a few days later, again:

> I stopped in all day, as I have got absolutely tired of St Tropez;
> it seems to be full of gossiping women, dirty children and
> men playing bowls. The only things I love here is the sea and
> the mountains, the latter near enough to see, but too far off
> to reach.

Eventually though:

> The people of St Tropez are beginning to recognise us and
> instead of staring, not a few pass the time of day. Only those who
> have lived in a place where it is impossible to comprehend what
> people are saying can know how welcome just 'Bonjour' is.

Like a gift later that evening, the ever romantic Grace discovers
that 'there is a new moon tonight, it is like an old friend. I wished,
I wondered, if that wish will come true.' By 5 November:

Another day has come and gone. The time flies by so quickly it is only another two months and we can be in dear old England; I shall feel like falling and kissing the dear old soil. I went to the pier, took a book and sat reading until 3.40pm, afterwards coming home for tea. Mrs Bell wanted some figs and finding they had all been eaten, looked at me as if she accused me of taking them. Oh I hate, hate it all. I wish I never had come, something always comes to damp my happiness. Tonight is Guy Fawkes Night. Oh How I long for dear old England, with all my friends.

But the following day the truth was outed: 'Julian had a very bad bilious attack from eating figs so it cleared that mystery up' and

the cloud has passed and I feel very happy again. Perhaps I misjudged Mrs Bell, any rate she has been very nice to me having given me some snap shots of Annie, Blanche and myself, also of the little boys. I was delighted.

The South of France was finally beginning to feel knowable too.

Nellie and I went to St Tropez this afternoon. The wind blew terrible, it was all we could do to keep on our feet. I must be a very eccentric person for my opinions are forever altering, for now I like St Tropez – not at all intolerable [and] I rather like my daily visit; in fact I look forward to it.

Luckily Grace had Nellie – much the same age – upon whom to rely for good cheer ('Nellie and I laughed so much I had a sore throat') and emotional support, although it seems she too fought off an understandable bout of homesickness that winter. They shared a birthday (4 November) – and that year it was Grace's eighteenth.

This morning was very hot, almost like summer. I felt very
pleased with the world in general and rose early. It was Nellie's
and my Birthday, I am eighteen years old. Therefore I feel very
old and important. My presents consisted of a shell necklace
given me by Julian, I felt very gratified to think that at last
somebody remembered me. I went for a walk to St Tropez after
lunch and sat at the end of the pier and surveyed the scenery
and watched the fishermen loading a cargo of logs. I saw two
enormous shoals of fish not unlike herring. After tea – chancing
to look up I saw a most hideous little reptile about eight inches
long on the wall; it was in a shape like a lizard. Its colour was
grey. Julian, Nellie and myself tried to catch it, but it proved
so very quick in its movements that after my chasing it all
over the house, we finally lost sight of it outside my bedroom
window. We afterwards discovered it was a species of Lizard,
very common in the South of France but quite harmless, called
a Gecko.

With such strange creatures in this strange new land,

Julian said he heard a wolf howl and was very anxious about
closing the shutters in case one might get in. I think it was a dog.

Grace too was not immune to frights. One night:

About 9pm had an awful scare: I went down to the woodshed
for some wood and had just got in when an awful rumbling
sounded inside. I let out a shriek and bolted outside. I waited,
then, summoning up all my courage I again advanced, taking a
stick and rapped on the door outside. The rumbling commenced
again, then a huge cat sprang out and disappeared into the
vineyard. It had sent all the wood falling and so caused the
rumbling.

Sometimes, even for a farm girl, the unfamiliar could stymie
plans.

Went fir-cone collecting after visiting the town after lunch. The boys came too, we found a huge goat chained over the place where we planned to go so had to retreat and collect chips instead.

One of the more enjoyable ways to reproduce the rhythms of London was evening visits to the cinema in St Tropez. Some showings were more successful than others, mostly due to the language barrier.

About 8.50pm Mrs Bell asked Nellie and myself if we would like to go to the Pictures. We both went and I enjoyed it very much, it was rather an interesting film; about a Brahmin god. Sorry we missed the first part and as it was in French we had to imagine most of the words … I don't think much of French Comedies. We arrived home about eleven thirty. Left movies still continuing.

One day was bright and warm, the next windy and cold. Trips into town were more and more fascinating, especially as Grace and Nellie were nicknaming the local inhabitants, who they believed to be swindlers at heart.

The wind has been simply awful all day and freezing cold. Went to St Tropez this afternoon and saw two destroyers and a big steamboat in the Gulf and had a small hope one might be English. But it turned out to be French. Arrived back in time for tea. Afterwards went to the Port to get some petrol; I went to one shop, the Proprietor of which told me to go 'a leetle farder'. So I went to the 'Powdered Girl who Spits' shop [and] she gave me some oil and took all my money enough to pay for twice the amount of oil. Mrs Bell is going to enquire into the matter. After tea a big spider lit on my arm, therefore I sang out and got severely reprimanded by Nellie, about pretending to be afraid.

Grace and Nellie's sense of being toyed with by the locals lasted well into November, for

> Nellie and I went to the Pictures in [the] evening, the Ticket woman trying to cheat us, saying we never gave her enough money. We were unexpectedly rescued by a Frenchman who spoke English, who afterwards made me very uncomfortable by looking round and staring me straight in the face; the kind of look that made you all quivery. Otherwise we enjoyed the Picture very much, arrived home about 12.30am.

Even mundane tasks appeared difficult here for 'after tea went shopping with Quentin, bought some bread, on the way home it mysteriously disappeared, so had to go and fetch some more'.

And one never knew quite what to expect when abroad. On one windy walk with Nellie and Angelica they were witness to

> an awful accident: a man was standing on a load of wood, when he fell off and in doing so got his head pinned between a cattle truck and wagon. Another man picked him up, the blood came from his eyes, nose and mouth and he would keep going back to the truck as it fascinated him. At last they managed to get him away and with the blood dripping from his face, all the way, marched him through the town.

The horror of such sights should have been mitigated by the joy of the town's children. On their way home,

> about thirty small boys attached themselves to us so we had the undignified honour of heading up a procession of grinning children, right up to the gates of La Maison.

But by the end of November older locals were beginning not only to approach Grace but also to speak a little too, for, 'On the way home [I] was asked by two French people of what nationality I was.'

On 23 November:

> We [Grace and Nellie] went sticking after lunch in the Pine
> woods, saw Louise who introduced two Frenchwomen working
> in the vineyards to me. I was not much impressed by them as
> they looked as if they could have done with a wash.

The following day, out again in the woods this time with Julian,
'a disreputable-looking Frenchwoman waved to me'. Snobbish
distaste virulently overtook Grace a few days later when out
fir-coning with Nellie.

> The Frenchwomen coming and bringing their families to talk
> to us. I am absolutely fed up with fir-coning and am not going
> anymore. Nearly all St Tropez was there picking wood and they
> all came and kept speaking to us and following us about like
> dogs. I hate it. I['m] not going there anymore.

Later in December she wrote that 'on our way home [we] were
disgusted by a man and woman with some goats'. Though she
was keen to learn basic French, Grace's conversational skills were
of course not up to local standards, which made most kinds of
socialising stunted and awkward. From now on Grace resolved to
buy the fir-cones in town, but that still required some interaction
with locals. It felt, however, more acceptable to grow frustrated
in purely economic transactions.

> I went for a walk with Nellie into St Tropez and bought
> some fir-cones and visited the Bazaar. The Proprietor of
> which showed us around. Nellie bought a ball for Angelica.
> Everything we touched the man packed up for us so we came
> out or he would have wanted us to buy the shop.

With few other places to go, the following day they were back at
the Bazaar, where Nellie bought a photo frame. Grace's anxiety

concerning the locals did not preclude attention to quiet details, for evidently she had noted, days or even weeks before, a small girl in the window of a local hospital. Coming home via the hospital, Grace writes that she saw through the window the 'same little girl in bed'. With Vanessa paying, that night Grace and Nellie 'went to the Pictures after tea'. But 'the film was a French one, all about murdering and the serials were all killing and poisoning, until I had the creeps'.

Grace's indifference, though, was sometimes challenged by the French:

> Went for walk up the road and visited the Chapel. A woman would persist in waving to me and when I took no notice she came to look [for the] reason and looked terribly angry at me.

Grace and Nellie's shopping for essential 'delicates' gave the St Tropezians something to laugh about. On 9 December:

> I bought some bloomers, I had a great difficulty in getting them and I did not know their name and there was a man in the shop, I had to talk to the man while Nellie went behind the counter and showed the woman hers. There was much laughter at our expense and whenever the wretched man saw me in St Tropez he came and whispered the French name for bloomers.

A few weeks later, buying stockings elicited no diary comment, so it would seem that Grace mastered either her French or her embarrassment. But her nerves could sometimes not be ignored, for only a few days before Christmas

> I went to St Tropez after tea for some bread, butter and biscuits [and] was suddenly taken with nerves and arrived home very frightened.

Duncan, though, could be relied upon as great company:

> After dinner Nellie and I went to the Pictures, Mr Grant went
> too and as it rained he borrowed Julian's overcoat. I do not
> think I ever laughed so much, as it reach[ed] not quite to his
> knees and fitted him so tightly round the waist, so as to show
> off his figure as if he wore corsets, and the sleeves reached to
> his elbows. I enjoyed the Pictures very much. Mr Grant walked
> home with us [and] we arrived home about 1am carrying two
> loaves of bread.

Duncan could even be enlisted to help with tedious domestic
chores, taking 'the washing on the push chair to St Tropez in
the evening'. A few days later Grace

> went to St Tropez to fetch washing from L'Hotel Zube, had
> an introduction to the worthy Madame Zube, but washing not
> arrived so we came home without and slept without pillow cases
> and in blankets not having any sheets.

The following day Grace went with Vanessa to L'Hotel Zube 'to
enquire about washing' though presumably it had yet to arrive.
So they went without proper bed linen for several days further.
It was on 11 November ('Armistice Day in England. St Tropez
celebrated by having a holiday and football match') that

> Nellie and I went to fetch [the?] washing, on our way call[ed] at
> a stationers to get some notepaper, getting into difficulties with
> [the] person in the shop, we were unexpectedly rescued by an
> English lady artist named Mrs Hazel staying at L'Hotel Zube. I
> found the washing in Mrs Fothergill's [Vanessa's local English
> acquaintance] room where she was endeavouring to dry Julian
> and Quentin's knickers. I felt very undignified as I marched
> through the square carrying a washing basket, as many of the
> crowd which frequent it on holidays turned and laughed after
> us. Mum sent me some Papers.

For Vanessa, Duncan and Roger, life was quiet, pleasant and full of painting:

> Weather warm, I went for a walk in the afternoon with
> Nellie and saw Mrs Bell and Mr Fry painting. Mrs Bell went
> for farewell Dinner with Mr Fry. Mr Grant in for Dinner,
> afterwards going to the Cinema.

After Roger's departure, December was heralded by dreadful weather.

> Rained terribly all night and day. I was all day bailing water
> from hall and dining room. The sea looks awful, lots of ships
> have taken shelter in the harbour. Nobody went out except
> the little boys to school. Louise [the French daily] in a terrible
> temper.
>   Maelstrom raging outside, the trees are all bending under the
> strain. The ships in the harbour are rocking awfully.

And soon 'we were all very Disturbed this morning to see snow covering the mountain tops, a very unusual sight as it never usually comes as far as Marseilles. I hope it does not fall here.'

By 10 December the weather had begun to improve and 'Mrs Bell went away for the weekend to Vence at Madame Bussy's'[2] returning as 'Madame Bell' on 13 December to continue her days of painting with Duncan. Grace may have been considering what to buy the boys for Christmas, for she records going into town and buying 'two serviette rings for Julian and Quentin'. Grace had caught another 'very bad cold and a sore throat' which only got worse in the following days, so that by 15 December (when Duncan departed 'for a holiday') the cold had been passed on to Angelica and Nellie so all were 'feeling rather bad'.

Angelica could not leave the house, and neither really could Nellie, and yet Grace, Louise and even Vanessa were desperately scrubbing the place clean for the expected arrival of the dreaded owner, Rose Vildrac.[3] And then, disastrously, on 18 December

> we had a fire in my room and got smoked so much we had to stand with our heads out of the window until finally rescued by Monsieur Santucci [the caretaker who lived nearby] who let us out.

But still,

> Quentin and I went to the cinema in the afternoon and were very gratified to find the words in both English and French, as we two were the only English in the place we felt sure it was for our own selves. The new serial very interesting is of the Revolution, by Victor Hugo.

By 21 December the Christmas anticipation was gathering apace:

> Nellie and I went for a walk into St Tropez and posted a letter to Mum with ten stamps on. Mr Grant still away. I had some books and papers with Xmas cards from Mum and kids.

The following day a card arrived for Grace and she notes 'the children very excited about hanging up the stockings'. Finally the expected day arrives:

> The weather was quite nice but very cold. Great excitement with Julian, Quentin and Angelica examining their presents. The boys gave me an Elephant and chocolates. Mr Grant a bottle of scent. Louise being away, Mrs Bell, Madame Santucci and myself cleaned out the kitchen and scullery. We had a Plum pudding and mince pies, roast pork, preserved fruits, dates, figs and oranges, also wine for luncheon. M. Landau[4] came for tea, they had a Xmas tree and Xmas cake and we had one. After we had a firework display.

Boxing Day brought the usual walk into town and Grace notes how 'people treated Xmas as an ordinary holiday'. The festivities soon over, domestic worries again demanded Grace's full attention:

> Louise in a furious temper, Mrs Bell having told her about the dirty kitchen. Nellie and I went for walk and there saw some English people who had just arrived for the winter.

Christmas week saw Grace elbow-deep in washing, with household anxieties mirroring the 'awful maelstrom raging outside'.

> Coming home I bought some fir-cones and for some unearthly reason the woman at the shop has taken a sudden dislike to me.

The cold weather, the work to be done and the local 'snub' meant that on New Year's Day,

> I stopped in all day, the Corsican coming with some wine taking us by surprise kissed Mrs Bell, then coming into the kitchen tried to kiss me. I managed to escape and was very upset. Mrs Bell told me it was the custom for men to kiss you on New Year's Eve. Nellie and I went to the Cinema and there saw the Polar [the Polish artist Rom Landau] and his friend Barmy, Frizzy Mop, Uncle Sam and the Click. Arrived home just in time to greet the New Year, which we celebrated by eating sardines in my room.

Grace led the New Year's Day expedition to St Tropez in search of fireworks to purchase, but they found little of interest. By 3 January:

> We were very busy all day as we [are] expecting Madame Vildrac tomorrow so I never went out. I hope she will not be so bad as Madame Santucci says she is, or it will be dreadful.

And the following day, the eagle landed.

> Madame Vildrac has arrived, putting us all into great
> commotion during lunch. She has yellow hair of the most
> extraordinary hue, a complexion which she makes herself and a
> very shrill voice. Mrs Bell in a terrible state, however the first
> day has passed and nothing awful happened.

On 5 January, Vanessa and Duncan kindly invited the Vildracs
to dinner. And two days later Grace was

> awfully busy packing, washing, and etc. At tea time Madame
> Vildrac came to look over the house, when she was upstairs
> what should Nellie do but break a lamp glass. Madame stamped
> down to enquire what was the reason, but luckily we had
> cleaned up the pieces and I went to St Tropez and bought a new
> one. Mde. Vildrac has terrified poor Mde. Santucci so much
> that she broke down and cried when speaking to Mrs Bell.
> Poor thing, she has been a sport to us, it is so cruel that she is
> treated so.

In the run up to their departure from St Tropez, Grace spent a
few days meditating upon the previous few months – and deciding
what a shame it would be to leave the place. To borrow a phrase
from E. M. Forster's *Where Angels Fear to Tread*, the South of
France had worked its 'pernicious charm' on her. Perhaps the
relaxed southern mindset affected her, because, either consciously
or not, she started the new year of 1922 by imagining herself a
month behind. So that on 6 'December' 1922 she writes 'only
two more days at dear old St Tropez'. The following day (still in
'December') some consciousness of loss sets in motion a desire
to hold on to what has been:

> It seems awful to think we may never come here again, never
> see our old friends, as we made many here, and never hear their

Grace (right) and Elise Anghilanti, the Bells' cook in Cassis,
holding Angelica and Judith Bagenal

old jabber (half French and half Italian). We might come again one never knows.

The day of departure is then correctly written as 8 January. And as they 'came away' from the town,

> a crowd of people came and saw us off at the Station including Madame and Monsieur Vildrac. M. Santucci [the caretaker], the Polar [Rom Landau], Barmy, Mademoiselle Bouvay [that is Bouvet, the boys' governess].

An assortment of friends came to say goodbye and Grace found she really was sad to be leaving.

Having taken some time to adjust to her foreign surroundings, she would for ever more enjoy such trips and mythologise them in old age. They became part of her education.

After arriving in Paris on 9 January:

> We stayed in Paris for five days at the Hotel de Londres. Saw Notre Dame, went for walks in the Tuileries Gardens and the Louvre, saw the old palace, went and bought costumes at Bon Marché and Louvre, and dined at the Continental Café.

Although Grace does not comment on the glamour of Paris, the simplicity of St Tropez stuck in her mind so much that she put pen to paper in the hope of clarifying the strangeness of her three-month adventure. In the twenty-seven 'Things I Noticed in St Tropez', she clearly reveals much about her own interests and concerns surrounding domestic arrangements, food, fashion, gender expectations and local customs:

> That the last thing Mr Fry takes off and the first he puts on,
>   before and after taking a swim, is his hat.
> The women here grow beards and moustaches and go bald.

That the men wear sashes, and use scent and powder, also the
majority wave their hair.

That huge Cactus grow wild.

That instead of corn, the French grow vine trees, and there are
pine forests covering a huge amount of land.

That cows drag their carts instead of horses and grow much
bigger than English oxen.

That the Frenchwomen wash at stone wash places and always
with cold water, and instead of soap, they mostly use the ash
of wood, after it had been burnt.

That the French very rarely use coal, mostly burning wood.

That nearly every person has his little vine-yard.

That the French men shoot all birds, including Tomtits, Robins
and Thrush.

The men in summer very rarely wear shoes or boots, and
sometimes not in winter.

The men's favourite game is bowls and cards.

That the pine cones contain nut, which are good to eat.

That there are numerous stone wells by the roadside which look
like holes till you look inside them.

That the cork oak abounds here.

That the streets are very narrow and also very filthy.

That there is a Cathedral in St Tropez.

That the Ladies of St Tropez have to wear veils, or they are not
Ladies.

That the people only keep Sunday till 12 o'clock, after that
spend the rest of the day in amusements and football.

That the Citadel on the hill was once a fortress.

That St Tropez has forty-two war memorials.

That the women have to carry the things and not the men when
out walking with them.

That the men do not take their hats off when in Public Places.

That the women sit mostly just outside their house to sew, in
summer and winter.

That sometimes when meeting they kiss on the cheek, both men
and women.

That women carry their parcels on their heads.
That the French women never make pastries, but buy them at
   the pastry shops.
Came back to England on 14th January 1922.

The return to England saw the Bell household pick up its usual
routine of life between London and Sussex. It was not until 1927
that Grace returned to the South of France with Vanessa and
Angelica.

They went to Cassis to nurse Duncan, who had been taken ill
there with suspected typhoid. They all put up at the rented Villa
Corsica and, with Duncan ill and Angelica in bed, the evenings
found Vanessa and Grace alone. Vanessa wrote to Clive that
Grace was taking meals with her, reading avidly and regarding
her alone as the source of wisdom for all things French. Vanessa
complains rather more revealingly, however, to Virginia, 'since
we have been here I have had practically to live with Grace – she
has had all her meals with us, generally alone with me in the
evenings, as it seemed too absurd for her to bring in my food and
then have her own rather later in the next room'.[5] It was during
this stay in Cassis that Vanessa encountered the English ex-pat
Colonel Teed. He and his mistress Jean Campbell lived at the
nearby chateau and owned a small farmhouse called La Bergère,
on which Vanessa excitedly took a ten-year lease.

Further trips to Cassis occurred the following year and in
1929, accompanied by relatives, artist friends and an assortment
of children. It was during the first trip to Cassis that Vanessa arranged for Grace and Angelica to be tutored in French by Madame
Chevalier (no doubt to get them out the way so she could paint).
Grace approached the task as confidently as any other. By 1928
she returned to Cassis and in a letter from Quentin to Duncan,

La Bergère, the cottage in Cassis
rented for ten years by Vanessa Bell

The landscape at Cassis on the
Mediterranean coast, twelve miles east of Marseilles

Grace with Angelica Bell and their tutor on the seafront at Cassis

written in April 1928 from Munich and now held by the Tate Archive, Quentin asks after the 'hectic life' at La Bergère and imagines 'Clive flirting with Grace or at any rate dancing with her to the gramophone'.[6] Further to such flirtations, by the spring visit of 1929 a live-in governess was installed at La Bergère who was also to be flirted with outrageously by Clive.

By the end of the 1920s, with Julian already at Cambridge and Quentin boarding at the Quaker school Leighton Park in Reading, Angelica too was sent away (in September 1929) to be educated at a girls' school in Essex. So in the last autumn of the decade – with the children grown and away – Grace entered another phase in her Bloomsbury existence. She would not travel abroad again for thirty years, was soon to be permanently installed at Charleston, and would shortly begin creating a family of her own.

FOUR

Style and Romance

Grace as a young woman

G RACE'S French 'debut' in 1921 offered the first recorded
example of her innate stylishness. Vanessa wrote to Clive
that Grace, adapting to the requirements of the warm weather,
was 'trapesing [sic] about in exquisite transparent clothes with a
handkerchief tied round her head, very lovely and quite incompe-
tent.'[1] Probably in the early 1930s – at the back of her 1921–22 St
Tropez diary – Grace jotted 'I was last in France in 1929. Stayed
in Paris, Lyon, Marseilles, Cassis.' These long visits were very
clearly remembered, for Grace deliberately and almost lovingly
wrote out all her French addresses:

L'Hotel Condrillon, Cassis, Bouches Du Rhone, France.
Villa Corsica, Cassis, Bouches Du Rhone, France.
La Bergere, Fontereuse, Cassis, Bouches Du Rhone.
La Maison Blanche, Route De St Anne, Var, France.
La Hotel de Londres, 3 Rue de Bonaparte, Paris.

She also noted in the same diary some names of interesting
people in Cassis. One is that of the distinguished Romanian
artist Lucian Grigorescu (1894–1965), a post-Impressionist painter

resident in Cassis and later elected to the Romanian Academy. It is claimed by Grace's son John, Duncan's friend Richard Shone, and Vanessa and Duncan's granddaughter Henrietta Garnett that Grigorescu asked the stylish Grace to marry him. Whilst there is no mention of this anywhere in her papers, her beauty and fun-loving disposition make it highly possible that he did propose at some point – most likely at Cassis in early 1929. The most likely reason she would not accept such a proposal was the simple fact that she was so young and he was a decade older than her. Henrietta Garnett is convinced that at some other point in the late 1920s or early 1930s Grace was proposed to by another Eastern European man – this time an aristocratic Polish Count – whilst sitting on the number 19 bus in Bloomsbury. John Higgens believes that Grace certainly wrote other diaries during the 'in-between years' (in other words the 1930s and 1940s) which she later destroyed, fearing they might upset her family. But perhaps we should not read too much into the mention of Grigorescu, for in the same list of those she met in Cassis is a German named (Walter) Becker, who is noted by Grace to have become a Gestapo chief.

On 28 November 1921 in France there is the first evasive reference to a love interest: 'On our way home saw someone we knew.' Now that she was eighteen and 'feeling very grown up' Grace's interest in men was increasing. And by 3 December the local young men had been given nicknames, not only as a useful way of recognising them but perhaps also as a way of mitigating the slight trace of nervous fear they engendered.

> Nellie and I went to the Pictures, Mrs Bell paying. Nellie saw her Bon-Jean and I saw Ted 'saucer eyes' and 'Polar' [Rom Landau] . Enjoyed films very much.

Style and Romance

The following

> very cold day, we went into St Tropez in our old rags and Lo
> and Behold all St Tropez was dressed up in silks and satins and
> a band was playing. Who should we run into but Bon Jean,
> 'Fuzzy Mop' and Barmy all in their best. Nellie and I hopped it.

On 6 December, whilst walking into St Tropez 'Julian and I met
the Spaniard'. On 8 December she and Nellie 'went into St Tropez
and bought a hat ... a lovely green one. Mrs Bell afterwards met
us and I bought some shoes.' The girls' critical eye was now being
cast over a collection of local lotharios:

> We went to St Tropez, on the way back saw the Spaniard in
> a rather awful position [perhaps Grace means he was bending
> over and showing his behind?], which greatly amused Nellie
> and myself. We went to the Pictures in the evening, where I
> saw Polar [Landau], also the Tabacs boys. Poor 'tea-saucer
> eyes' looked rather squashed and we did not look at him.

And a few days later, despite having a cold, 'Nellie and I went to
St Tropez and there saw the Tabac boy who tried to follow us,
but we misled him and got away.' Playing games and teasing the
local boys became their speciality. By 17 December,

> I went shopping and in the Grillon met a boy who could
> speak English a little, so he practised a little on me. Julian and
> Quentin much mystified over my French young man.

An increase in basic French was rivalled by an increased confidence
in her alluring power over men; indeed one is not required to
speak much when flirting. And only a few days before Christmas,
she writes 'saw the Polar with another Gentleman'. On Christmas
Eve,

Nellie and I went to the cinema and saw the Polar but the little
Bon Jean was not there. The film was inclined to be boring
as it was religious tableaux. The serial of the Revolution very
exciting.

On 29 December 'Nellie and I went for walk into St Tropez,
saw the Polar and a friend.' On New Year's Eve, she saw him
again at the cinema. Grace and Nellie thoroughly enjoyed playing
flirtatious 'catch me if you can' games with Landau and his friend.
They clearly understood their own attractions and hence their
power over men. At the bay side on 2 January 1922,

a French officer came up to me and enquired if I were admiring
the scenery, in perfectly good English, after that he wanted to
come part of the way back with me, but I managed to give him
the slip and came home alone.

Poor Nellie, demonstrating her age and innocence,

had a most funny adventure with Polar this morning. She
met him in town and he insisted on accompanying her home
and on the way asked her to go to the Cinema with him. She
arrived home looking terrified and stopped in all day and done
washing.

The handsome, intense-looking 'Rom' Landau was evidently
charmed by both young ladies and was happy to be seen with
them:

Nellie met the English Lady this morning and also the Polar,
and had a formal Introduction to him from the Lady.

Naturally it was Grace's appearance – her hair and her clothes
– that concerns her most in the early diaries. Clive is recorded
as buying her books; Vanessa bought her clothes – affectionate,

A formal portrait of a young Grace

motherly and possibly controlling gestures: 'Mrs Bell came back from Paris & bought me a new voile dress ... very pretty.' Back in London, with board and lodging always taken care of, Grace was able before her marriage to spend much of her earnings on herself. Whilst they may have been meagre, what little she had was her own. From London on 13 March 1924 she wrote:

> I have bought a ripping little hat, black trimmed with red
> patent, now I want a coat, Oh so badly. I wonder when I should
> get one.

And somehow, by 24 March, she had been to the department store C&A and bought one:

> I went out & bought a new spring coat, a very nice one with
> a ruffled collar & straight frills half way up the coat & on the
> sleeve.

She believed appearances were important, so that even when a pressing tea-time obligation required speedy dressing, 'I took rather a long time to dress so we arrived about an hour late', even though it meant her host was kept waiting.

> Today is Sunday, it is a very nice day, such a day that you
> feel you want to put on all your new clothes if you had any &
> parade to Church in them so everyone can see them.

Preparing for an extended trip to Sussex, she wrote on 4 April 1924 that 'I tried to do my hair up, but never succeeded so think I will have it cut anyway', and comforts herself that 'I have a decent pair of crocodile shoes which I shall take to the country'.

Richard Shone recounts how on a bus from Lewes in the spring of 1924, Duncan once almost mistook a young Grace and middle-aged Mrs Harland (the cook) for the great style icons of the day, devastatingly chic socialites Lady Diana Manners and Lady Sybil Colefax. Playing dress-up for fun was part of life at Charleston in the early days, and in that same spring, Grace wore with great panache a pair of Julian's breeches, his shirt and Duncan's big straw Spanish hat,[2] a vision Richard Shone remembers Duncan describing as 'too ravishing for words'.

Life rolled along, full of the usual joys and anxieties. Her employers noticed her beauty and it affected her life with them – often against her own wishes: 'Mr [Clive] Bell came in to lunch & as usual said some very idiotic remarks making me feel very uncomfortable.' We cannot know what it was that Clive expressed, but given Grace's charms – and the other maid Alice's anger noted later in this entry – we can reasonably imagine it was flirtatious. Grace and Clive remained on affectionate terms throughout their lives. On 16 April 1924 Grace wrote, 'I had a lovely Easter egg from Mr Bell with a lovely pair of silk stockings inside' and decided not to tell Alice for fear of her jealousy.

Duncan too appreciated female beauty, and he could not help admiring Grace, once sweetly sending her a Valentine's card (which she always treasured). He wrote,

> Grace looks more exquisite every day. She wore a red
> handkerchief with white spots on her head yesterday and I
> think I may make a sketch of her to put into a picture.[3]

Frances Spalding recounts how, at a royal film premiere of J. B. Priestley's *Good Companions*, Duncan thought Grace 'looked far smarter than most of the ladies present'.[4] And Vanessa herself commented on Grace's beauty: when Louie Dunnett took over as Angelica's nanny in 1923, Vanessa wrote that although Louie

A Valentine's card sent from Duncan Grant to Grace

was suitable 'she isn't half as aristocratic as Grace'.[5] Years later, and as a family intimate, Grace was even invited (along with the Queen and Princess Margaret) to Westminster Abbey for the wedding of Duncan's young friend Lindy Guinness to Sheridan, Marquess of Dufferin and Ava. In later life Grace looked neat and handsome. In youth her attractiveness was a sort of feminine currency which could, however, cause tension in the kitchen at Gordon Square:

> I had my hair waved & it looked lovely, everybody kept telling me so & Mrs Harland [the cook] was mad, especially when Mr Harland [the handyman] said so. She was jealous; a catty thing to say, but it is true.

Naturally fun-loving, Grace was also aware that Bloomsbury's affection for her occasionally depended upon an element of performance:

> I dressed up in Julian's trousers and Quentin's jersey & had my snap taken, I then walked to Swingate ... in them.

Buying new clothes and meeting eligible young men were connected, of course, and were equally thrilling pursuits for a young woman: 'bought a hat, it is quite charming. All black with a black Georgette streamer. I had tea at Lyons ... with the violinist in the orchestra.' Perhaps Grace's earliest 'beau' was Edgar Weller, a labourer who lived close to Charleston, and drank in the local pub, the Barley Mow, which is probably where they initially met. For much of 1924 he appeared to want more from Grace than she was prepared to give:

> I have been trying to write to Edgar, but I really do not know what to say, as he is so serious. He talks of settling down &

I am sure I cannot settle down and as for housekeeping I am sure I would be a perfect ass at it. I think I will write to him and ignore all that part of the letter.

Except he really wouldn't give up:

I had a letter from Edgar, I do not want him, do not know how to give him up, he is so serious. Rats to know all men.

Edgar sent me a lovely box of violets & thanked me for a letter which I have not sent ... Mrs Harland [the cook] had the grumps.

Am frightfully bored at present & have got to write to Edgar, men are a nuisance.

Coming home [from the Barley Mow] I had a row with Edgar. He asked me to marry him & I said no, I did not love him.

Edgar came & proposed for about the eighth time.

... the postman asked me if he could write to me.

Grace's good looks were no doubt inherited from her own mother, known as Old Mrs Germany and remembered as 'very handsome' on her infrequent visits to Charleston.

On a crowded London tram to Teddington in Middlesex to stay with her uncle and aunt for the weekend, Grace records this conversation with the conductor:

Tram Conductor: 'Miss, will you marry me? I have been looking for a wife & I think you would suit me'

Grace: 'Oh have you?'

Tram Conductor going up to a staid looking old Lady with a huge bunch of lilac:

'Madam, would you give me a bunch of flowers? I would like my young lady to have a bouquet when we get married'.

The Old Lady very confused, turns & gazes out of the tram window.

When I got off the tram conductor told me I should really
pay another penny, but as I was marrying him I need not.

Whilst at the Lyons teahouse on Oxford Street with Mrs
Uppington, Grace

> met Captain Neil [whose identity is now unknown] who asked
> me to have coffee with him, but I refused.

A few days later at London's Kingsway Theatre with Mrs
Harland,

> I met Captain Neil who asked me to go for a motor ride with
> him. I refused.

Evidently he was another persistent admirer:

> Captain Neil came round & caught me in the kitchen. I never
> spoke to him. I went for a walk with Louie, Alice [another
> housemaid], Judy [Bagenal] & Angelica, we met some staff
> officers. Coming home a Sergeant asked me to go out with him.

With such resistance one can imagine how she grew more attractive. Her sense of propriety insured her charms – particularly in
the closed world of rural Sussex.

> Tom West [Charleston gardener's son] insulted me by saying
> that Edgar Weller slept with me last Easter which was a great
> lie. I called his father over & told him. He very severely
> reprimanded Tom who cried & came & begged Pardon.

It seems, though, that young Tom was himself rather in love
with her:

> Tom West told Mrs Upp he was my young man & tried to kiss
> me, there upon I called upon God to let me die & he could not
> kiss me & gave it up as a bad Hope.

> I am a beast. I have not written to Edgar. Poor Boy it shows
> I do not love him.

And eventually Edgar tired of the chase, marrying instead Ruby Coles – later housekeeper of fifty years to Maynard and Loppy Keynes at nearby Tilton. 'Ruby Coles went out with Edgar Weller, whom she told me she hates (why need she lie?).' Edgar was perhaps never quite what Grace hoped or imagined he should have been:

> If only everyone knew how I always despised Edgar & how he
> used to bore me, I used to loathe being left alone with him.

On 4 July 1924 even his last letter to her appeared to be something other than it was.

> Had a great shock. I thought I had a cheque, but when I opened
> the letter found it was from Edgar giving me the sack. Thank
> Heavens.

Grace's attitude to lovesick men was like that of a mother to a silly child.

> I just now had a fright, as I sat writing this diary. Alice came
> in with an orange, I had just enough time to hide, otherwise
> she would surely have wanted to read it. Louie in terrible form,
> having just received a letter from Eric the boy she does not
> want, telling her all she has missed & how wrong she is. I told
> her not to take any notice, that he has not much pride or he
> would not keep writing as she has already told him three times
> she does not want him. She thinks her mother's persuaded him
> to write.

Still, to most male visitors she was always 'darling'. The one man by whom she would have liked to be described as such was the

Grace in the garden at Charleston

handsome and gay Sebastian Sprott (1897–1971), briefly a lover of Maynard and tutor to the Bell boys during the early 1920s.

> Mr Sebastian Sprott came to stay with us for the weekend on Saturday. I love him (he looks so clean & big).

The most significant relationship of her life, however, is not covered by the surviving journals. Upon her marriage to Walter Higgens he was made head gardener and she housekeeper, thereby securing their permanent home at Charleston. Like Grace, Walter Higgens was bred of farming stock and had a variety of local labouring jobs throughout his career. At one point his parents left their farm and bought a pub in the village of Alciston, just beyond Tilton Wood, which was said by Grace's daughter-in-law Diana Higgens to have been 'drunk dry'. Exactly how he and Grace initially met goes unrecorded, but it is unlikely to have occurred here. As we know although she was never a great drinker she would often accompany her colleagues to the local Barley Mow pub, so it is possible she initially met Walter there. Or perhaps he delivered livestock or dried goods to Charleston's kitchen door? We will never know. But, according to their son John, Grace and Walter's marriage proved an affectionate one lasting nearly fifty years. To commemorate their wedding day (26 May 1934) Duncan gave them as a present his painting of the Colosseum in Rome – a quite magnificent gift, the ancient marvel perhaps intended to symbolise enduring marital strength. A quiet and gentle man, during the First World War Walter served with the Hampshire Cyclists and, according to his son, proudly proclaimed on his return home that he did so 'without ever firing a shot in anger'.

Unusually for the 1920s, Grace did not have her ears pierced, but she did possess a collection of round and brightly coloured clip-on earrings. Indeed, according to Diana Higgens, a set of these was the first thing she put on in the morning. And following convention, in public she always wore a hat and gloves right up until her retirement in 1970. The conventional public uniform of hat and gloves marked her out as a professional woman worthy of public respect and admiration. When worn by Grace, this 'uniform' of staid respectability went further. Her innate understanding of style, often described by Duncan as 'exquisite', meant that even in the thin blue housecoat she wore every day at Charleston, she appeared more vibrant than the average Sussex housekeeper.

Vanessa Bell holding her son Quentin

FIVE

A Brave New World

Grace with Angelica and an unknown child

M OST OF US SUFFER, from time to time, with what Winston Churchill famously described as the 'black dog', and Grace was no different. After a winter in St Tropez experiencing the daily vividness of life in the Mediterranean, returning to chilly London cannot have been pleasant. It appears to have set in motion a cloud of boredom which in turn became a kind of youthful ennui and a depression of sorts; for by the end of April 1922 – just when one might imagine the spring to sweep such feelings aside – Grace turned to the private space of her diary in desperation:

> I am going to continue my diary as I cannot remember all that happened during the months since I came back from France [so] I must leave it out, and start from today. Nothing very interesting has happened.

The following day 'I felt very bored all this evening' and again 'my boredom is increasing and not decreasing'. By 29 April,

> I was so bored this afternoon I nearly went mad my head ached. I feel as if I want something so very much, yet I do not know

what it is. It makes me feel sick inside. I do not wonder that people commit suicide, or even murder. Life sometimes grows so monotonous there is no wish to live. I sometimes think, 'I wonder if it would hurt if I killed myself?' then another time, I am terrified at the sight of a knife or a needle in Quentin's hands, as he is so fond of pretending to push it into me. I wonder if it is how some crimes are committed; the same thing every day, nothing to change, the monotony until one feels one must do something or go mad, then someone comes in while one is in this mood and in desperation you crack that someone over the head with something. The mood passes and you come to your proper senses to see the awful thing that is done. Then comes the discovery by the police, the trial and found guilty by the jury. The death. All because [of] the monotony of Life.

Taken out of context Grace's words can begin to sound like abstract modernist poetry.

Work as usual ... Work just as usual ... Done as usual ... Done as usual in morning ... Done as usual ... Done work just as usual ... Just as usual ... Just as usual ... Rained all day.

And the monotony does not go away. Her feeling of being trapped, unsure of herself, unable to move either forward or backwards, mirrors perhaps the feelings engendered by that black monkey in a window on Tottenham Court Road.

Today is Sunday and my fit of depression is still upon me. ... All the afternoon I wanted to cry, and I sometimes feel I should faint. I wanted to go out and when Mrs Bell said I could, I did not want to go.

Happily, by May Day 1922, 'at last the fit of depression has gone and I feel better', though when out walking, 'my stocking persisted in falling down and I arrived home feeling very uncomfortable'.

The enjoyable times make Grace's innocent life sometimes sound like that of a girls' boarding school, particularly when the household staff were moved *en masse* to visit other houses or when Bloomsbury figures came to stay and brought their own staff.

> A tremendous thunder storm last night; Louie terrified fetched Alice & I to sit up with her & I went to sleep on her bedroom floor.

Such intimacies were necessary and comforting. During these visits Grace would often have to share her room or bed with an opposite number. Virginia Woolf's high-spirited maid Lottie Hope was often thrown together with Grace, her contemporary: 'Lottie slept with me & told me lots of her most extraordinary doings & I told her some of mine.' Tantalisingly the diaries do not record Grace's 'extraordinary doings', so we can only imagine. Midnight confidences often helped to stave off loneliness, and bound the staff together in more positive ways:

> I stayed up rather late talking with Mrs Harland & laughing over my adventures at St Tropez. I came to bed wishing so very much I could go there again.

She and another housemaid 'signed a pact that we will both go abroad in the beginning of next year'.

The reasons surrounding her fit of depression can be guessed at. A great deal of her life was directed in some way by her social superiors (Vanessa, Clive, Duncan) or professional superiors (the elder servants), perhaps leading to frustration over a lack of personal control or liberty in her life. For a girl who grew up during a devastating war, life needed to be lived to its fullest and its fairest. But for Grace it felt as though nothing had changed for the better. Her diaries bring the frustrations of monotonous domestic life vividly into focus, for the kitchen contained a group of disparate people, young and old, forced to live in close quarters and undertake arduous and monotonous labour. On 29 February 1924,

> Louie had the diarrhoea & a rotten headache ... Mr Harland arrived home slightly intoxicated. He has just drawn 10 weeks wages. Emily [fellow housemaid] has broken 2 small bones [in her hand].

And the following month:

> Today was lovely & scenty, with Oh such a lot of dirt & work, poor Mrs Upp felt very bad & Mrs Harland had the grumps, so altogether we are a very miserable houseful.

Sometimes petty squabbles and grievances rose to the surface. On one such occasion in April 1924, 'Annie [cook] was very upset and looked as if she would dissolve in tears'. Territorial tensions were exacerbated, particularly in the kitchen, and Grace naturally used the privacy of her diary to vent her feelings:

> I do not like her [housemaid Alice] much, she is very affected & has a very great imagination, especially concerning herself.

But when in London she was often able to escape a few doors away to lunch with the Keyneses' servants. To the naïve Grace, confidences – perhaps shared late on a Saturday night after a drink – were often shocking or amusing or both; 'we were entertained by hearing some more of Alice's immoral doings'. But the morning came and it was always an early start: 'Sunday is always the busiest day.' The diaries consistently reveal how the young Grace's fantasies are kept in check by a rather mature grasp of reality. The world was a divided place.

> I gazed upon the wonderful creations in [presumed department store] Thompson & Shoolbreds windows and wished them mine, but what's the use of wishing. One rarely gets what one wishes for.

As well as entries which express how 'it's good to be alive', often she used her diaries as an open forum to express her outrage at the gulf between the interwar haves and have-nots. Walking home via Old Compton Street in Soho,

> A poor woman selling violets came up to us. She said she had 3 children and wanted to get back to them. She looked so thin and hungry, I think it is wicked some have so much and others so little.

The streets of London provided the kind of radical political education that would have been almost impossible in the rural Norfolk of her childhood.

> As I was going up Hampstead Road [on Shrove Tuesday] I saw an instance of what some of our ex-soldiers have fallen into. A man & little boy of about 5 years old poorly but neatly dressed stood outside a shop. The little boy looked like a little skeleton dressed up. His little legs were so thin they could not hold him up, so that the poor man who looked nearly as bad had to hold him up.

As a sometime nanny in a wealthy household, the sight of poverty-stricken homeless children evidently affected her deeply: 'I could cry each time I think of that poor little baby's face, all bony with red rimmed eyes.' In the early 1920s, the fate of ex-servicemen was much debated and Grace was not unaware of the struggles facing the urban poor and dispossessed.

> I think it is wicked to let our poor men come down to this …
> I get so mad. I wish our rotten old government would blow
> up [as] it keeps wrangling over its own silly affairs & let all
> the poor men who fought for them starve. The only time they
> remember the poor is when there is a war & they are in too
> much of a funk to fight for themselves. Then they make up the
> poor to do their dirty work & make promises which they never
> mean to fulfil.

Grace's political radicalism went deeper than might have been imagined by anyone who knew her in her polite old age. Even 'below stairs' such views caused surprising friction and upset with the older middle-aged servants who aligned themselves with the status quo:

> I had a row nearly with downstairs about my awful socialist
> views. Mrs Harland thinks that the poorer classes never ought
> to be allowed to raise themselves up, never ought to be allowed
> to get into Parliament. I think that the poor are on the same
> level as the rich & some superior in Brains.

She is expressing the views of a postwar world that would – within her own lifetime – become widespread, especially after the Second World War, and which would make possible the reforms of Clement Attlee's Labour government. Of particular distaste to Grace was the implication that socio-economic control was equated with sexual control, regardless of the consequences:

> Mrs Harland also thinks that if a wealthy man offered to make
> advances towards a poor girl, she should be honoured & allow
> him to do whatsoever he liked with her, for the few miserable

shillings he would condescend to bestow on her. And also she should be able to brag about it, that she had been mistress for one night or a few weeks or months of a man with money.

Grace evidently held the ancient conviction that a woman's greatest pride is her virginity and sexual abstinence:

> Also she [Mrs Harland] thinks I am mad because I said if a rich man wanted me he would have to marry me, for if I was mistress to a man & he turned from me to another woman, I would kill him. And she also says I am mad because I said I do not want to get married, as I would lose my independence … and I do not like men only as pals.

The older Mrs Harland's opinion was markedly different – perhaps it was born of a harder life. As seen in the last chapter, Grace's virginal conviction and fiery passion proved irresistible to many men. Full of youth, beauty and a vibrantly straightforward 'feminist' spirit, Grace had very much her own opinions on the modern man:

> I think modern men think too much of themselves; they think a woman ought to jump at the chance if they offer to marry them & I hate them for it.

Just out of her teens, Grace deliberately placed herself in opposition to her colleagues:

> You see I love contradicting people. If they praise them I see their bad points, if they run them down, I see their good. I simply cannot help it.

Recognising the contemporary conflation of modernity with madness, and buoyed no doubt also by the example of her 'betters' upstairs, young Grace was happily complicit in the Bloomsbury rejection of traditional political status quos.

I told her [Mrs Harland] if she was sane I would rather be mad
for I am far happier than anyone downstairs ... They all think
I am mad because I cannot look like them [or think like them],
and I am so glad I am mad.

Like many young people after the First World War, Grace experienced a deep yearning for something better, a desire to destroy
the bonds of 'murderous' monotony, but the solution eluded her;
the power to change things was still vested in those with the
economic means to do so.

I stayed in all day and felt very lonely. I have a restless longing
which I do not know how to satisfy.

Whilst Vanessa was busy renegotiating the terms of modern
womanhood by working independently, travelling and loving
freely, Grace was simultaneously trying to redefine what it meant
to be working-class in this new post-war world. Both women at
different periods in their lives sought to reshape what it meant
to be what they were. In a letter to her sister Virginia, Vanessa
writes about the 'curious ... lower class mind':

Though extraordinarily nice and free from any of the tiresome
qualities of many of our friends, she [Grace] is, like all the
uneducated, completely empty-headed really, and after a bit it
gets terribly on one's nerves. She asks me questions, which it is
obvious she could answer as well as I can, or she tells me things
she has already told me dozens of times about the Harlands.
One has practically no ground in common. I am rather
interested to see what does happen with the lower classes, as
Grace is a very good specimen, not only unusually nice, but
much more ready than most to try to understand other things,
reading all she can get hold of and making desperate efforts
towards culture. But there's something I suppose in having

educated grandparents, for already Angelica is capable of understanding things in a way one can see Grace never will.[1]

Yet Grace always knew how to pull herself back cheerfully from any sense of bitterness, instinctively deprecating her vulnerabilities in a very English way:

> In the evening I was so depressed ... I was so miserable I cried myself to sleep. I am an ass.

By the 1930s she and her employers had to 'grow up'; the political situation in Europe could no longer be ignored by the household – or indeed, before long, by the nation. Ideological conflicts were looming in Europe and the Bell household could not avoid being affected by them. A passionate Communist, Vanessa's elder son Julian served as an ambulance driver with the International Brigade in the Spanish Civil War and was killed aged only twenty-nine in 1937. A trusted family intimate, Grace discovered Vanessa 'weeping in the garden one day because no one realised her need to talk about Julian'.[2] In later life, Grace cited Julian's untimely death as the only bad thing to have happened during her fifty years at Charleston. Even as she grew older, and as her horizons inevitably narrowed, Grace never lost her empathetic ear, her wise good sense, her cheering smile and her appearance of being completely unshockable.

Julian, Angelica and Quentin Bell

SIX

Charleston

L IFE for the servants at Charleston was spartan but pleasurable and often full of laughter:

> I spent an exciting half hour watching Albert Ford & the rest of the farm hands chasing a cow with its calf which persisted in going in the wrong direction.

Freed from the sometimes earnest atmosphere of Gordon Square, in Sussex Grace's benevolent employers felt rather more like friends and were often the instigators of merriment:

> Louie & I stopped in all evening. Duncan Grant the Artist, thinking to frighten us dressed up in some weird clothes and hobbled about. Louie thought he was a cow, Mrs Vanessa Bell was very amused.

The servants themselves were often dressing up or doing impersonations, sometimes pushing the older members of staff beyond the point of comfort:

> Arthur West [a gardener] 'did' The Rotter. Mrs Upp so amused she made water & had to go upstairs.

Arthur's son Tom was also a local joker:

> Tom caused very great amusement by helping me to wash some
> clothes. He dressed in an overall of Alice's & a hat of Judy's,
> also wearing Mrs Upps spectacles.

The warm and relaxed atmosphere of Charleston encouraged
the breakdown of social barriers, so that very occasionally the
house must have appeared to local outsiders as something akin
to a rural commune.

> Last night Arthur West, White & Kemp [both local soldiers]
> climbed Mr Grant's window & tried to get in his bedroom. I
> beat them out.

It is unlikely that Duncan was occupying his bedroom at the time,
but even if he had been, he would have seen the fun of it.

The popular perception of Virginia Woolf as a melancholy
neurotic is challenged by the obvious delight her family often
took in her presence:

> Mrs Woolf arrived after tea to the great joy of the household, as
> she is very amusing & helps to cheer them up.

Sixty years later, Grace even described Virginia as 'very frivolous'.[1]
As for other members of the Bloomsbury Group, Roger Fry could
be unreliable, for Grace writes that he 'was going to take Angelica
to the zoo. But he never came for her', and the biographer Lytton
Strachey is described as 'a very peculiar man of Moods'. Indeed,
sometimes she struggled to understand her social superiors:

> I met Mr & Mrs [Adrian] Stephen [Vanessa's brother and
> sister-in-law] coming down Francis Street. They were arm in
> arm & laughing together [as] if they had not one care in the

world. Who would think that they were living apart and that
Mr Stephen was broken hearted & had considered taking his
life. Perhaps it is only talk, I mean the broken hearted part, but
[I] think they are very peculiar people.

The Stephen family (Vanessa, Virginia and Adrian), though well
to do, were generally rather scruffy and unkempt, and Grace's
reactions to them sometimes reveal her youthful aspirations to
la vie bourgeoise. In old age she said in an interview that 'I never
thought of them as being particularly talented. It was just their
way of life.'[2]

> I met Mr & Mrs Leonard Woolf riding on their bicycles
> to Charleston, they look absolute freaks, Mr Woolf with a
> corduroy coat which has split up the back like a swallow tail &
> Mrs Woolf in a costume she had had for years.

The touching details of daily life at Charleston allow us the chance
to witness the growing of children and maturing of adults:

> Julian, Mr Bell, Mrs Bell & Mr Grant tried to teach Quentin to
> ride a bicycle, Mr Bell giving [an] exhibition performance, but
> to no avail [because] Quentin gently but firmly refuses to throw
> his leg over the crossbar. I laughed very much to see them, it
> was as good as a pantomime.

The compelling romance and nostalgia associated with rural life
during this interwar period is vivid.

> After dinner about 10.30 Louie & I went moth catching with
> Julian & Quentin & got a record haul off one tree, besides
> getting our feet drenched with dew.

One spring weekend with the children was particularly active
and rewarding too:

I climbed the [Firle] Beacon with Louie, Angelica & Judy
[Bagenal]. Julian & Quentin very set on my climbing the
Beacon to see the sunset tomorrow Sunday morning. I arose
very early & climbed the Beacon at about 5.30 am with Julian,
Quentin & Louie to see the sunrise. We arrived at the top long
before it came up. All the clouds turned a gorgeous Salmon
Pink, there after many false alarms the sun rose. We came back
by the winding path and arrived back at Charleston, after Julian
Quentin & I had paid each other extravagant compliments,
about 7.30.

Sometimes though, as we know, there was a good-humoured
tension existing between Quentin and Grace:

Julian & Quentin came into the kitchen & as usual Julian,
Quentin & I got very personal & paid each other very
uncomplimentary remarks. Julian however is very complimentary
and is turning into a gross flatterer.

It appears from Grace's diaries that the adolescent Julian had
something of a crush upon her. Here he figures – one suspects
– as the gnat itself:

Louie, Julian, Quentin & I held a séance in the boys' bedroom.
We put all the lights out and sat holding hands in the dark
(Julian at least seemed to enjoy this part of the performance). It
came to an abrupt conclusion however. As I sat there something
flew between my legs and bit me, therefore I shouted & lights
were brought. We could not find the wretched creature which
bit me. That ended the séance for the evening.

Summer evenings in Charleston, particularly in the 1920s, were in
some ways more social than in London. Within walking distance,
the Barley Mow, mostly populated by local farm labourers, figured
highly in the staff's merry-making:

> In the evening I went up to the Barley Mow with Alice & there
> saw Mrs Upp, Roma, Ella, & Edgar Weller, Lionel Pelling,
> Ruby Coles, & Mrs Harland. They all looked very surprised to
> see me. Ella & Roma played the piano. Everyone got hopelessly
> drunk except Roma & I. Mrs Uppington kindly drank all my
> wine for me. I had to lead her home while she persisted in
> telling everyone what a nice girl I was. Charlie White & Arthur
> West walked up the drive with Alice & I. Charlie White would
> kiss me good night. Paul [farm hand?] very angry. I disgraced
> myself by going into the Barley Mow, but he bought me a box of
> Peppermint Creams, and Louie & me have forgiven him. Amen.

Even into this idyll, modernity came crashing, quite literally into
the lane at the bottom of the Charleston driveway when Grace
witnessed a motor accident:

> It appears a motor car ran into a milk lorry, then rebounded
> back into a hedge. No one was hurt, but our lorry man was
> very much shaken up.

Grace preferred to observe the boozy merriment from the sidelines,
rather than to participate. In the hot summer of 1924 she writes
that, after a staff day out with the children at Eastbourne,

> I came to bed early & heard Alice, Mrs Harland & Ruby
> singing as they came home from the Barley Mow.

The youthful Grace became the subject of Vanessa's famous
painting *The Kitchen* (now hanging on the upstairs landing at
Charleston), which expresses a cheerful and earthy rusticity
and reflects Grace's crucial role in the household (after all, no
other servant was asked to sit for a portrait). According to John
Higgens, Clive Bell even dispensed regular financial advice so that
Grace 'played the stock market all her life'. Although she always

Vanessa Bell's painting 'The Kitchen', c. 1943

regretted her lack of formal education, she was a well-informed newspaper reader, and during the evenings, Duncan, Julian or Quentin would often bound into the kitchen and ask Grace to return with them to the dining room and give her opinion on a particular subject or political event of the day. Writing to Grace from the Continent in the early 1930s, Vanessa comments that 'everyone asks after you and is anxious to know when you are going to be married. I cannot tell them'. And later, 'I wish you were here.'[3]

By the early 1930s Grace was the only live-in servant at Charleston, and upon her marriage in 1934 – against the domestic conventions of the earlier twentieth century – Grace was kept on and made housekeeper. When Grace and Walter Higgens became engaged, he was working on a farm just off the Lewes Road at Milton Street and they were offered a tithed cottage in which to live. But Grace thought it desperately primitive, and resolved with Vanessa that they would stay living and working at Charleston. Perhaps, then, Walter had little choice but to become gardener at Charleston. There was always work that needed doing and he was paid an extra half crown a week to clean out the chickens. Vanessa unkindly referred to Walter as 'the Dolt'. In some ways he was a threat to the stability of her household; after all, he might easily have insisted on a move elsewhere. Vanessa wrote to Julian that Walter as gardener is 'rather obstinate but hard working – and completely ignorant – at any rate about flowers'.[4] Many, it seems, were surprised when Grace became engaged to him; it was thought she could easily have done 'better'. Walter was a quiet and amiable man, a voting Tory, who was, despite Vanessa's opinion, good with his hands. As a gardener he proudly won local prizes for his 'apples and gladioli' but, according to John

Higgens, he ultimately disliked some of Vanessa's demands (for example, asking him never to pass in front of the dining room window when guests were staying). Later tensions concerning his work in the garden eventually led to his finding better-paid day jobs elsewhere on local farms or in the nearby brick and cement works.

When Grace finally did marry Walter, a telegram was dispatched from the Continent that read 'Love, congratulations and best wishes from Vanessa Bell and Duncan Grant'. Virginia Woolf too wrote an affectionate note from her London home at 52 Tavistock Square:

> Dear Grace, Mrs Bell has just told me that you are actually married. So we want to send you our best wishes & congratulations. Will you buy yourself a present with the enclosed, which comes with our love & we hope to see you at Rodmell. Yours, Virginia Woolf.

On 23 May 1934 Vanessa wrote warmly from her London studio in Fitzroy Street (along with the wedding present of a cheque for an unspecified amount):

> I am so glad that I need not write to say goodbye, but only to send you every affectionate good wish from us all and hope that you will be very happy and make yourselves a lovely home. Yours affectionately, Vanessa Bell.[5]

Interestingly, Vanessa's correspondence and manner became more affectionate after the Higgens' marriage. Perhaps she worried that to become too close to a servant girl would encourage socially inappropriate confidences and ultimately imply greater responsibility for Grace on her part. Once married, Grace safely became Walter's responsibility. At King's College, Cambridge,

51

From **Virginia Woolf**, 52, Tavistock Square, w.c.1. *Mus.* 2621.

29th May 1934

Dear Grace,

Mrs Bell has just told me that you are actually married. So we want to send our best wishes, & Congratulations. Will you buy yourself a present with the enclosed, which comes with our love, & we hope to see you at Rodmell. yrs. Virginia Woolf

A note from Virginia Woolf to Grace

there is a rare letter from Walter held in the Clive Bell archive, written at this time:

> I am so glad that although I am married, I am still living at Charleston, it is very kind of Mrs Bell and yourself ... I hope some day to be able to repay the many kindnesses to which I am indebted to you both.

Grace could easily have taken her marriage as a conventional excuse to leave the Bells, and the fact that she did not shows how happy and valued she felt with them. Durning Vanessa's extended travels in the South of France and Italy during the late 1930s Vanessa wrote jolly, friendly letters to Grace which implore her housekeeper to 'write and tell me how you are getting on and all your news'. After over a decade in service to the family, Grace was trusted and depended upon more than ever. Vanessa often trusted Grace to take on extra duties that might be associated with those of a secretary or personal assistant, such as opening telegrams and dealing with them 'as you think best', making telephone calls on Vanessa's behalf, and forwarding letters to both her and Clive.

During Grace's pregnancy in 1935, Vanessa wrote from Rome and sent 'my love and best wishes'. A few days later Duncan kindly wrote 'please let me know when I can come and see the baby', signing off affectionately 'yours always'. By the middle of May Duncan wrote to Walter, rather than Grace herself, and asked that Walter 'please congratulate Grace for me' upon the birth of their son John, and soberly signed off with a 'yours sincerely'. Vanessa wrote again to Grace from Rome in response to Walter's formal letter announcing John's birth:

> When you're well enough and have a minute to spare do send me a short letter to tell me about yourself and the baby as you know men aren't much good at describing babies.[6]

Grace holding her baby son John (1935–2013)

Grace even received a letter from Duncan's sympathetic mother Mrs Ethel Grant (then living at Twickenham), who fussed over baby clothes to be bought by Duncan as a present, and who signed off 'with best wishes to you both, yours truly'. Interestingly Vanessa wrote again from Rome to say that:

> Perhaps it will be best if you don't try to do anything for us, but lead a separate life. What do you think? I expect John Peter [the newborn] gives you plenty to do. I'm longing to see him and hope he goes on being so good.[7]

Even Virginia Woolf at nearby Monk's House in Rodmell found Grace endlessly reliable, typing sweetly onto her husband's headed stationery:

> Many thanks for the delicious cake which we both enjoy every day at tea. Could you be so good some time as to write out the recipe, as I can't get any cakes made except yours that I like to eat? We go to London tomorrow. V. Woolf.[8]

With Vanessa and Duncan away for most of that winter, the Higgenses and their young son John lived at Charleston alone: an idyll if it weren't for the cold and damp.

By the late 1930s a relative formality had again entered into Vanessa's correspondence with Grace (who by now, regardless of Vanessa's movements, remained entirely in Sussex as house-keeper). But sometimes the letters are chatty and feel neighbourly in tone. From Perugia, and comparing the food there with her favoured French dishes, Vanessa encourages Grace to go abroad for her holidays with Walter:

> I really think you ought to go at least to Dieppe [a short ferry journey from nearby Newhaven] simply to eat. It's so easy, we

52

From **Leonard Woolf, Monk's House, Rodmell, Lewes, Sussex.**

Many thanks for the delicious cake which we
both enjoy every day at tea. Could you be so good
some time as to write out the recipe, as I cant get
any cakes made excpet yours that I like to eat?
We go to London tomorrow.   V. Woolf.

A note from Virginia Woolf to Grace

got there in no time from Charleston, one could hardly believe it, and then you'd get just as good food as in Paris and it's a very nice old town and you could bathe on the beach.

By this time Vanessa's letters contain a generalised anxiety about the international situation. On the eve of Hitler's invasion of Czechoslovakia she writes to Grace from Fitzroy Street:

We are naturally all rather agitated about the news here and you must be too. I do hope things will calm down soon. One simply doesn't know what to think or expect. The world in general is certainly mad.[9]

Vanessa lived at Charleston full-time for less than three years during the First World War, and between the wars the house was effectively a part-time retreat. It was not until 1939 that Vanessa began living more permanently at Charleston, and she undertook several renovations including the addition of a sitting room for Grace and Walter just off the kitchen. Only days after the signing of the Munich Agreement, Vanessa wrote from La Bergère in Cassis:

We got here two days ago just as the news was at its worst and found everyone in despair in fact all the way through France everything seemed to be getting worse and worse, with so many men being called up and having to leave their families war seemed almost certain. It's a great relief to hear better news and everyone is cheerful.[10]

She wrote again to Grace on 10 October:

I am sorry you had to cut short your holiday I think we were lucky to be out of England though it was bad enough in France and we didn't know what difficulties one might have in getting back. I cannot help feeling thankful for a short time of relief from the strain of expecting war though everyone seems to think we must prepare for it once again I suppose the sensible thing to do would be to grow as much food as possible at a place like Charleston vegetables, pigs, ducks and all we can. Anyhow it could do no harm and we might be very glad of such things as one would have been in the last war. But we cannot really make up our mind to another calamity. It's so lovely here it seems absurd that people cannot be left simply to enjoy it … One picks as many grapes as one can find to eat [and] the whole place seems running with wine.[11]

A great deal of Vanessa's work held in her London studio was lost as the result of a fire in a bombing raid, but otherwise she and Duncan were not unduly affected by the war, and with Walter growing vegetables and Grace rearing the chickens, Charleston became a self-sufficient haven amidst the general privation. Vanessa wrote to Jane Bussy[12] during the summer of 1940 that she had 'driven the Dolt with such an iron rod all these months that we really have plenty of cabbages … Poor man, I have no mercy on him.'[13]

Neither Vanessa nor Grace was given formal schooling, and their writing hands take idiosyncratic turns that often ignore the conventions of spelling and punctuation. Vanessa's writing style, particularly, gushes from the page in a flurry of haste and excitement in a rather adolescent way – or, as Richard Shone believes, in a style typical of painters. The tone of Vanessa and Grace's face-to-face conversations was probably affectionately formal and their letters do not substantially deviate from this established standard. Beyond the housekeeping arrangements, the discomfort of wartime, the weather, their health, the health of those they knew and the behaviour of the children, there were no other points of common interest to be discussed.

The 1930s were the decade of Grace's coming of age, with marriage, motherhood and the heavy weight of Charlestonian responsibility. At eight o'clock every morning guests were woken by a cheery Grace, who drew the curtains and left a jug of hot water on the nightstand. Never having waited at table, Grace had breakfast (as well as lunch and dinner) waiting in the dining room ready for the family to help themselves. By nine o'clock Grace would be seated at the large scrubbed kitchen table with her pencil and notepad, and Vanessa would sit beside her to give orders for the coming day. After Grace's sitting room was built in 1939, the nine o'clock orders were given there, as regular as clockwork. Vanessa had early experience of running an old-fashioned Victorian household, managing the servants at her parents' London home, 22 Hyde Park Gate,[14] and her manner could – according to Grace's son John – prove 'austere'.

Vanessa's lifelong diligence as a householder naturally extended to precise accounting, and Grace's chief anxiety was in making sure grocery bills from Firle Village Shop were kept within budget. This goal was often attainable, with the house and the garden proving almost entirely self-sufficient: vegetables were grown and livestock reared. Grace was a keen gardener herself, and in addition Leonard Woolf would often give her vegetable roots for the garden and cut flowers for the dining table. Over the years she kept many geese and pigs; within living memory there were two geese named Mr and Mrs Jones and a pregnant sow called Hannah. When their time came a local farmer would take them away to be killed before bringing them back to hang in the Charleston pantry. The farmer's wife sometimes assisted Grace in the curing of their meat or in the plucking and skinning of Clive's regular brace of pheasant, snipe and rabbit. Logan

Thompson,[15] the Keyneses' farmer at nearby Tilton, would often kindly bring in more game to be hung. One of John Higgens's earliest memories is of the blood dripping from these carcasses onto the old newspapers neatly laid out on the floor of the pantry. Indeed, John claims that salting the pork cured him of his warts. Grace and her family were by now knitted into the very fabric of Bloomsbury. Four-year-old John posed several times for Vanessa in her attic studio and became one of the small boys in her paintings *Nativity* and *Annunciation* in nearby Berwick Church. No doubt Grace recommended her younger sister Alice Germany as maid to Maynard and Loppy Keynes, and although Alice was briefly employed at Tilton, she 'didn't take to it' – according to John Higgens – and ultimately returned to Norfolk.

Charmingly, cows from the fields would often stick their heads through the kitchen window, and Grace welcomed their curiosity. Alongside the daily dusting, sweeping, scrubbing and mopping so essential to good housekeeping in a busy home, Grace would regularly go out into the local hedgerows to pick blackberries for jams and preserves and into nearby woodland to pick mushrooms for cooked breakfasts or luncheon soups. During the afternoon lull Grace took great pride in tending the narrow flower bed beneath her kitchen window. As company, Grace and Walter had a dog of their own, a collie called Blotto – a relation of the Keyneses' own farm collie in fact – with whom Vanessa shared a birthday (30 May). Blotto's kennel was a former beer barrel in the garden. During the week of Blotto's death, Duncan, writing to Richard Shone, mentions how sad the household was. A country girl by birth, Grace loved animals and often tenderly warmed found or damaged birds in the kitchen oven before hopefully returning them to a sheltered spot in the garden.

Grace was a natural reader and always found the time to read the vast pile of newspapers on the kitchen table. Occasionally dinners lasted well into the night, so Grace was required to wait until the family and their guests had finished and gone to bed before she could clear the table, do the washing up, and re-lay the table for breakfast. Perhaps it was during these evenings that Grace did all her reading. However, particularly in the later years and in deference to Grace, Vanessa and Duncan were strict about leaving the dining room at nine o'clock sharp. Twelve hours later the breakfast table would be ready for the morning rush.

During wartime there were sometimes disputes, as Vanessa recorded in her letters:

> There have been terrific domestic upheavals. Lottie[16] got at odds with the Higgens family (Grace and the Dolt) and our sympathies were divided. But when it came to the point of loud shrieks during dinner and terror lest a carving knife should be brought into play something had to be done. So finally Lottie went, and the Higgens family remain, but have a separate ménage of their own. Grace in fact has become a daily, and in consequence I cook the evening meal. The result is most of my stray thoughts are given to food, and in spite of all this I must say we live very well.[17]

There were moments of sometimes awkward fun, particularly during the great relief of Victory Week in 1945. Somewhat unkindly, Vanessa recounted to Angelica that on the second day of celebrations they all went to Tilton 'in a downpour at 8 o'clock' to find

> an enormous straw figure of Hitler with a ghastly papier-mache head made by Q[uentin] having been carted there earlier, and we were given beer and biscuits and cheese, and all the farm attended and the Higgenses and lots of small boys, Wests and Wellers, etc. Then songs, with a painful episode of songs by the

D[olt] which reduced nearly everyone to ill-suppressed giggles. He assured us with deep passion and very flat notes that he would stand by us whatever befell. Poor Grace hid her head in the background. But almost the worst moment was when they danced and the D[olt] seeing Edgar [Weller] waltz round gallantly with [his wife] Ruby, tried to do the same by Grace, who simply sent him packing. I never saw him so crestfallen.[18]

John Higgens attests that the 'only time I ever saw Mrs Bell smile was on VE day' when she had been unexpectedly kissed by Charlie, a Cockney chef who worked at a nearby army camp.

By the 1950s domestic work had theoretically become easier. Grace was naturally keen on the cheap new labour-saving devices, but had trouble persuading Vanessa of the benefits of linoleum. Concessions were made, however: a new oven was bought, Clive installed a refrigerator (in order to 'cool his gin and tonics', according to Grace's daughter-in-law Diana Higgens), and a vacuum cleaner was bought for the carpets – although Vanessa apparently found no other sound more annoying than that of vacuuming in the dining room. In the interwar period all Charleston laundry was 'sent out' to Lewes but by the mid-1950s a new washing machine had been bought, thereby making all laundry the responsibility of the now middle-aged Grace. By the time of the Coronation in June 1953, the Higgenses had their own television in Grace's sitting room. With Duncan and Vanessa in London, the great event was watched here by Grace and her family along with some of their friends, while the local farmers watched through the open window. With interior improvements came exterior deterioration. The flint-and-chalk road to Charleston was, by the late 1950s, becoming so impassable that local tradesmen refused to deliver, which meant that Grace had to walk further and further afield for the odds and ends required by the ageing Vanessa. But naturally Walter needed Grace too. Vanessa writes to Angelica that:

> Our only news at Charleston was that Grace, jumping up in a rage with the D[olt] (so she said) at 3 A M, rushed to get him some dyspepsia tablets, stumbled at the top of their stairs and fell all the way down on her behind – and then fainted – and then John [their son], hearing the noise, rushed down and fainted too. The Dolt I imagine lying comfortably in bed all the time. However they came to and went back to bed, but Grace appears to have cracked her spine. Not as serious as it sounds apparently, as she has been X-rayed and is getting better … But it was very painful for some time, especially when sitting down.[19]

Vanessa and Duncan's granddaughter, the writer Henrietta Garnett, cannot remember life without Grace, and describes her affectionately as a 'pillar of my growing up'. Sent by her parents, Angelica and 'Bunny' Garnett, from their home in Huntingdonshire with strict instructions to be 'very good for Grace', Henrietta spent many childhood holidays at Charleston, being cuddled to Grace's ample bosom when tearful, bounced upon 'charming' Walter's knee, taught how to iron the frills on dolls' clothes, helping in the kitchen, and listening to Grace reminisce about her own Norfolk childhood. Strikingly, Henrietta now believes that Grace was 'more maternal than my own mother'. Another of Vanessa's granddaughters, the artist Cressida Bell, fondly remembers how Grace's kitchen was always a 'haven' for young children – who were banned from the studio, naturally excluded from adult conversation elsewhere in the house or simply bored by Duncan and Vanessa's beloved radio serial *Mrs Dale's Diary*.[20] Grace always had time for the young Bells: she enjoyed talking with them and encouraged them to assist her making cakes and puddings for her famous teas. For Henrietta, Grace 'always smelled delicious' and, when pressed to remember her exact scent, immediately replied: 'of moist, homemade fruitcake'. In Henrietta's memory Charleston was idyllic, and in her dreams the house is still the safest and happiest place in the world. This emotional memory of Charleston is in no small part a direct result of the love and stability Grace lavished on the house and its visitors.

Walter too is well remembered by Henrietta, who describes him as 'a honeypot; very kind, very good, and always – and I must emphasise this – very funny; he was a lot of fun – they both were, Walter and Grace.' Indeed, she believes the reason Grace stayed at Charleston for fifty years was partly because 'she loved the larks' to be had there. Cressida Bell describes Grace as the 'solid base' upon which everyone in the family relied. Rejoicing in children and having also nursed Angelica, Grace cared for Henrietta and would eventually be of great help looking after Henrietta's own daughter Sophie. Henrietta recounts how, on a visit to Charleston as a young widowed mother, getting up in the night to attend to Sophie in a long nightgown made for her by her own mother Angelica, her sleeve was trapped in the electric fire and caught light. Before she could panic, Grace, apparently sleeping just below, appeared with a bucket of water – always 'an angel' manifesting herself at the right time, whenever she was needed.

To Henrietta, the plain fact was that 'under the auspices of Vanessa, Grace ruled the roost'. Frances Spalding has described how theirs became a relationship of 'mutual respect and dependence'.[21] But Cressida believes that there was a price the Higgens family paid for this relationship; that there was a degree of 'sublimation' on Grace's part – for whilst she freely and happily

Walter and John (1935–2013) Higgens

mothered Vanessa's children and grandchildren, Walter (sometimes described by the Bells disparagingly as 'Mr Grace') and John appeared often as silent or invisible presences at Charleston. There was a sense in which Grace 'divorced herself' from her own family, demarcating an emotional line between them and her employers. There was of course a clear border between Grace and Vanessa themselves – sometimes quite literally. Vanessa wrote to Duncan in 1930 about putting up curtains in her studio to solve the 'Grace problem. I don't mind hearing her as long as I know I'm inviolate.'[22]

While Vanessa could sometimes be chilly, Duncan was quite the opposite, and would regularly go into the kitchen for a chat with Grace and her family, often helping out and generally proving himself something of an emotional support. In this way his attitude to servants was very different from Vanessa's – perhaps because it was not his job to give the orders. In the words of Diana Higgens, Duncan had 'the human touch'. He proved himself to be a friend, and together he and Grace would often potter around the local plant nurseries. Diana Higgens recalls a day in the early 1960s when she offered to drive Grace to her doctor's appointment in the village of Alfriston. They went home via the Barley Mow, where Diana drank far too much to drive home and Duncan came to the rescue with coffee and a strong arm. One of the funniest and most charming accounts of life at Charleston concerns Duncan driving Grace on local errands in Vanessa's motorcar. Both suffered from what Virginia Woolf described as the whole household's 'sublime ineptitude' when it came to cars. After one outing when seatbelts had been introduced, the two of them had to find a garage to advise them upon how they might release their seatbelts, having spent hours trying. Never a driver herself, Grace often endured Vanessa's own idiosyncratic skills at the wheel. On one drive from Sussex into central London, they stopped at a crossroads, and when it was their turn to move they simply couldn't do so, and spent a good deal of time trying to discover why. Eventually it was pointed out by a passer-by that Vanessa had forgotten to take off the brake.

According to her son, Grace was a voting Liberal. During the summer of 1967 the Conservative politician Edward Heath particularly annoyed her by turning up hours late to a lunch at Charleston that, by the time he arrived, was stone cold. Easily exhausted by this point in her life (she was sixty-four), she often complained to her son and daughter-in-law that 'I'm so tired, my legs hurt'. The many heavy burdens of a decaying old house and the care of ailing Duncan sometimes became too much for her. According to Richard Shone, when returning to Charleston a day early from her holidays sometime in the late 1960s, Grace found that another of Vanessa and Duncan's granddaughters, Nerissa Garnett, had thoughtfully modernised the kitchen by fitting a new draining board and curtains. In surprise and exhaustion, and with a degree of proprietorial feeling, Grace walked through the door and simply burst into tears. It was the only time Richard Shone can ever remember Grace crying during the period he knew her.

But it was Grace's palpable warmth that really stuck in the memory of those who knew her. From La Souco in 1960 Vanessa wrote to Jane Bussy (daughter of Dorothy Bussy, Duncan's cousin),

> Grace, who gets in touch with everyone, has been talking in some peculiar language to the old people below and makes them give her oranges and grapefruit and anything she wants.[23]

A few days later, Vanessa wrote again to 'Janie' concerning Grace and the Bussys' housekeeper Madame Otto, who is

> charming and kind and seems to understand our wants very well indeed. What language Grace talks to her I don't know, but as usual with Grace's acquaintances I expect they will become fast friends.[24]

Back at Charleston tradesmen were always received into the warm kitchen for early-morning tea and chatter, and it became something of a morning tradition for Grace to welcome the local postman too. Cressida Bell describes Grace's kitchen as 'the hub of Charleston'. Much to Vanessa's consternation, on Christmas Day 1946 Grace invited three local German prisoners of war to celebrate with her and her family at their meal around Charleston's large kitchen table. Many years later one of these men returned to visit her with his wife, presumably in part to thank her for past kindnesses. Grace's generosity and sympathy here are a striking example of E. M. Forster's wartime maxim to choose personal relations over patriotism.

SEVEN

Legacies

Duncan Grant, 1968

A FTER suffering from pleurisy for nearly a year, by January 1960 eighty-one-year-old Vanessa was robust enough to take the train to France with Grace and Duncan for a holiday at La Souco, the villa at Roquebrune belonging to Duncan's Bussy cousins. Clive, staying in a hotel at nearby Menton, thought it was a fairly grim holiday for all concerned; Vanessa refused to leave the house, Duncan was anxious and Grace overworked (as well as lacking an allowance, having had it cancelled by Vanessa for the duration of the holiday). In fact this turned out to be Grace's last trip to France, as well as Vanessa's – she was to die the following year.

On 7 April 1961, when Vanessa was suffering from bronchitis, Grace wrote:

> Mrs Bell much worse, not able to move, Doctor does not expect
> her to live through the night, but so brave, when the doctor
> asked her how she was she said much better, her breathing is
> terrible, Ringmer nurse came this evening to help me make her
> bed & change her nightdress, Quentin took [his son] Julian to

London & came back. Angelica coming on midnight train. Mr
Grant trying so hard to keep her alive, feeding her every hour
with spoonfuls of Brands extract.

It was later that night 'Mrs Bell died at midnight' and the following day 'I shall miss her terribly.'[1] As ever, the tone is affectionate
but not intimate. Even on Vanessa's deathbed class boundaries
were respected. Grace had offered Vanessa forty years of practical
comfort and stability. Behind many influential figures of the past
there was no doubt an expert housekeeper, taking care of the
mundanities of life in order that their employer's thoughts might
be nurtured relatively unfettered by the daily grind. It seems,
therefore, no coincidence that Quentin and Duncan's descrip-
tion of Grace as the 'angel of Charleston'[2] so obviously echoes
Coventry Patmore's Victorian poem concerning the 'Angel in
the House', an idealised figure Vanessa and her sister Virginia
associated with their long-dead mother.[3]

Even in 1968 the eighty-three-year-old Duncan was still giving
Grace an occasional cheque 'to pay for an outing to see some
interesting place' – a kind, almost grandfatherly, gesture. At this
advanced stage in their lives Grace was partly acting as Duncan's
secretary as well as his housekeeper. Grace, though approaching
retirement, continued to produce delicious meals, to bottle fruit
and to make jams, jellies and marmalade. Under her rule, the
kitchen was always warm, the Aga well stoked and a smell of
fresh coffee in the air. The concrete floor was mopped daily and
the walls and ceiling regularly whitewashed, a task she undertook
herself. Duncan's dependence on her is reflected in the letters he
sent her when abroad, which, in tone and detail, were identical to
those he had sent Vanessa. He dreaded her brief disappearances.
For the most part Grace was a constant yet unobtrusive presence.

Her respect for Duncan's privacy left him able to invite whom he liked to Charleston.[4]

The issue of retirement threw up a conflict for her because of the great burden of responsibility she felt, not only for Duncan but also for the house. She had battled bravely, in the house and garden, against encroaching decay, but that year she admitted to Duncan that it was more than she could cope with. She was persuaded to stay on but, partly in order to give her a rest, Duncan arranged to spend almost three months of 1968 abroad.[5] As a late Christmas present Duncan, unable to get out to go shopping, gave Grace and Walter a cheque for ten pounds (never cashed). In many ways, though, Grace was taken advantage of: in the autumn of 1969, tired out by the labour needed to keep Charleston going and wanting to retire, she issued a second ultimatum. The artist Barbara Bagenal (1891–1984), an old friend of Duncan and the Bells, was present at the time and, foreseeing that things would be very difficult for Duncan if Grace left, she made Grace promise to stay on. She did so, but from now on Duncan tried not to have too many visitors staying at once.[6] When Grace was asked by Quentin during an interview recorded in 1969 what she remembered of Charleston in the early days, the 'lamps and candles' immediately sprang to her mind. There were many more servants and gardeners then, of course, and yet there was always a 'great deal of work'. Her role had changed: 'I've been sundry different things.' She remembered an 'old gentleman' who used to come and pump water from the outside pump-house. She remembered visitors such as Osbert Sitwell, T. S. Eliot, and Julian Huxley, who had a 'wonderful voice, rather like Roger Fry's'. There were 'many happy times', the only 'bad time' being Julian Bell's death. Grace's early memories of the South of France

were evidently very strong and very fond, and one can feel in
her soft tones the magic of those winter holidays in the sun. Her
life at Charleston was approaching its close and this brought out
an uncharacteristic nostalgia. In the same interview she mentions
Peter Pears ('he lives with Benjamin Britten and is a very famous
singer') and that Peggy Ashcroft came to Charleston for lunch.
In February 1970 she turned on the radio and

> listened to the life of Marie Lloyd & remembered Walter
> Sickert the painter at a Dinner party in 46 Gordon Sq[uare],
> singing 'My Young Man is Sitting in the Gallery' ... Listened
> to a radio script about Sir Frederick Ashton, remember seeing
> him on a summer afternoon leaping about Charleston Lawn
> with red Roses threaded in his hair.

The following year when E. M. Forster died she noted how,

> I remember him staying here when we had a fire behind the
> Kitchen Wall, & the fire engine came out; he was very amused.

Not long before her death she wistfully said in an interview that
'they were all my kind of people',[7] which no doubt explains why
she remained working for them for so long. Retirement finally
came towards the end of February 1971, when Grace was sixty-
eight. Duncan threw her and Walter a melancholic champagne
send-off in the drawing room.

More than a decade earlier Grace had bought and renovated
her parents' farmhouse at Banham in Norfolk, expecting to retire
there. But, deciding against it, she now sold up and bought for
their retirement a bungalow in Ringmer, a village not far from
Charleston. It was at this time that Charleston seemed to Frances
Spalding to have become 'like a place for ghosts'.[8] And yet the old
connections were kept up, with deeply affectionate and gossipy

Grace shopping at Firle Village Stores

Walter and Grace Higgens

letters frequently sent to Grace from Angelica and Quentin with 'very much love' to all the Higgens family.

Perhaps the saddest letter in the British Library collection is one of the last addressed to Grace, written in May 1975 by Duncan's old friend Clarissa Roche, wife of the poet and academic Paul Roche (1916–2007). According to (Paul and) Clarissa's family, the letter reveals Clarissa's anxiety concerning the elderly Duncan's safety and comfort under the auspices of the somewhat chaotic housekeepers who replaced Grace during the early 1970s.

> Dear Grace,
>
> It was so very nice to see you again. And it was a great pleasure to have a private tour of the 'Grace Collection'. I came away feeling rather dreadful for having been indiscreet. I really shouldn't have talked the way I did about the present ménage [Duncan and his new housekeepers]. I know you won't say anything – though it must be obvious to everyone. I simply felt badly that I may have upset you. To me the past and the present at Charleston is very symptomatic of the times, and it distresses one no end. There won't be much of a place for decent people in the future. One can only thank heaven you have lived when you have, and could create a very distinct role in a corner of the world.
>
> Our love until we see you again, Clarissa Roche.

Such a letter as this demonstrates the importance of Grace's role in Duncan's life. She did indeed carve out a distinct role for herself in an unusual corner of the world. Henrietta Garnett has said that for Grace (as well as herself) 'Charleston was an education – who needed school?' Henrietta also asserts that her grandmother Vanessa's only house rule was that whatever bed-hopping went on at night, residents and guests must be back in the right bed by the time Grace woke them with a jug of hot water in the morning. This was genuinely out of respect for Grace as well as to preserve a modicum of decency. Although Grace was careful never to make it known, she must have understood exactly what was going on. At some point too she will have understood for herself that Angelica was actually Duncan's daughter and not Clive's. A naturally compassionate woman, she was unfailing in her discretion – an ideal servant. Her surviving diaries make no mention of her employers' complicated relationships, and even in old age Grace spoke publicly about how she always got 'really angry when people talk about their lives and how they used to go to bed with each other. I was never aware of that sort of thing going on.'[9] Of course, servant gossip had repercussions, and Grace could have lost her job for speaking too freely. But much worse would have been to land an employer in prison by disclosing his homosexuality. Grace was far too loyal to Duncan to take any chances and defended him in this way even after his death. Her steady grip on domesticity mirrored her firm grip on professional discretion. This loyalty proved itself over fifty years of unstinting devotion and reflects well upon the surprisingly urbane and unshockable Grace.

> They were my sort of people. I was very fond of them all. They were just ordinary people who never interfered with anybody else ... I never thought of them as being particularly talented. It was just their way of life.[10]

⤳

Vanessa and Grace were both do-ers – strong-willed women with little formal education, sensitive to beauty, possessed of mountains of energy. One was born with money and the other was not. On a daily basis, Grace and Vanessa relied on one another, and in the opinion of many who knew her Grace was very much 'moulded' by Vanessa: aesthetically and domestically, of course, but also culturally and politically, by being freely offered important books.

Knowing how much she was needed, Grace was happy to stay on at Charleston when she could easily have left. According to Henrietta Garnett, Vanessa always 'kept useful people around her via a sort of umbilical cord'. Vanessa was an employer and always considered Grace, before anything else, as an employee. Theirs was essentially a transactional relationship. Beyond that there was a reserved affection tempered by mutual respect. According to John Higgens, fear played its part too, for even in later life – after years of companionship – Grace was sometimes anxious about Vanessa's imperiousness. Neither woman would have let a misjudged word slip or crossed the unspoken line of class convention. Henrietta Garnett concurs: 'If the line is crossed all integrity is lost.' Nevertheless, Henrietta tenderly describes their relationship as an 'extraordinary act'. There was a 'faithful collusion and complicity' between Vanessa and Grace, a 'mutual devotion'.

It is fascinating to 'see' some of the Bloomsbury Group through the eyes of a young servant girl. Albeit fleetingly, her surviving diaries and letters provide a charming and immediate insight into daily life at the heart of Bloomsbury, giving colour to some of the thoughts, feelings and aspirations of an ordinary working-class girl in the interwar period. Thanks to her surviving papers Grace has now become part of the Bloomsbury legacy. Although her diaries were written privately and were never meant to be read by anyone, they do readily enable us to identify with her. In the 1920s Grace could never have imagined they would prove of wider interest today. Only later, in retirement as a Bloomsbury 'treasure', when approached by researchers or journalists, did she realise her perspective might prove significant. If there is anything in her son John's suspicion that his mother destroyed some of her more private musings, perhaps this is when she did so. Her busy life as wife, mother, housekeeper and friend no doubt often got in the way of diary writing – the silence required for it was happily drowned out. And really, why would that have bothered her?

> It is awful, but you know I have forgotten what happened on Friday, you see I am so dilatory ever to keep anything up that I start, so I quite forgot about my poor diary until today, but I remember some of the things that happened between the days.

Epilogue

Grace in the garden at Charleston shortly before her death

Today is so good I am full of fizz, I have told everybody it's so
good, in fact that's all I can think of.

17 April 1924

I N   M A N Y   W A Y S the experiences of Grace's daily life echo those
of thousands of ordinary working women of her generation.
In other, significant ways, they do not. Her lifelong proximity
to both Vanessa and Duncan lends her papers a significance
they would not otherwise enjoy. Yet her legacy is crucial to the
Charleston story. Grace's youthful voice is genuine, and spoken
through diaries that are as unselfconscious as they could be. Even
in her old age and long after both Vanessa and Duncan had died,
Grace was protectively defending their public reputation against
gossip and scandal; thrilled to know her opinion mattered. Her
devotion to Vanessa and Duncan is touching to hear recalled, and
after Vanessa's death no-one could fill the void she left behind
at Charleston. With Walter pottering about the garden, Grace
and Duncan spent several quiet years together. In many ways,
this was Grace's closest relationship. Both Duncan and Grace

spent their lives in orbit around Vanessa, and both had to pick up the pieces when the 'Queen of Bloomsbury' died. There was a mutual sympathy between Duncan and Grace arising initially from their innate sense of fun. On a deeper level, a gay man and a working-class woman were both outsiders in the traditional sense, and perhaps that fact too, in time, solidified a subversive bond – another 'collusion', as it were.

In retirement at Ringmer, Grace's return visits to Charleston were wrenching affairs and sealed the already potent sense that the best of times had been and gone. Duncan, sensitive and alert as ever, was now as aged as the house, and Grace noticed the details of their decline: dusty shelves, unwashed floors and threadbare carpets, all beyond her control. On Duncan's death in 1978, he thoughtfully left Grace £300 in his will.

> I did not expect it ... I did not think the poor dear had much money. But it is nice to be remembered ... Bless him, I still cannot feel he is gone.

It is telling that, having bought and renovated her childhood home in Norfolk, at the very end of her working life she could not bring herself to return there. Sussex was her home, her son and his family were close by, and it seems Charleston was the unmovable epicentre of her world. The value of a life can be reflected in the memories one leaves behind – and if this is the case, then Grace's life was exceptional. Henrietta Garnett and Richard Shone have both said, independently and on entirely separate occasions, without a hint of self-consciousness and brimming with heartfelt conviction, 'I'd have done anything for Grace.' The artist Cressida Bell has a stronger mental image of Grace than she does of Duncan or even of her own father, Quentin. To this

Grace at Charleston

day Charleston brims with Grace's presence, and her kitchen is forever blazing with visitors, chatter, affection and purpose. Aside from her family and the papers she left behind, Charleston itself is Grace's primary legacy. The achievements Vanessa and Duncan fought for owe an indescribable debt to Grace – the woman, as it were, behind the canvas.

Notes and References

Notes

INTRODUCTION

1. Vita Sackville-West, quoted in Victoria Glendinning, *Vita: The Life of Vita Sackville-West*, p. xi.
2. Writing about the modern cook of the 1920s ('a creature of sunshine and fresh air'), Woolf compares her with the Victorian cook of her childhood who 'lived like a leviathan in the lower depths' of the house. *Mr Bennett and Mrs Brown*, p. 5.
3. Virginia Woolf, *Between the Acts*, p. 29; an allusion to Shakespeare's *Troilus and Cressida*, and Wordsworth's 'The Old Cumberland Beggar'. 'Scraps and fragments' neatly sums up Woolf's last novel, in which, interestingly, Grace briefly appears as 'Grace', the servant at Pointz Hall who brings the tea-tray to a daydreaming Mrs Swithin (p. 7).

ONE

1. Clive Bell (1881–1964) studied at Trinity College, Cambridge, with Vanessa's brother Thoby Stephen (1880–1906), Duncan's cousin Lytton Strachey (1880–1932) and Virginia's future husband Leonard Woolf (1880–1969). John Maynard Keynes (1883–1946), E. M. 'Morgan' Forster (1879–1970) and Roger Fry (1866–1934) were all at King's College. All were members of the Cambridge University discussion group known as 'the Apostles'.
2. E. M. Forster, *Howards End*, p. 134.

3. (Adeline) Virginia Stephen married Leonard Woolf on 10 August 1912.
4. Simon Watney, *Bloomsbury in Sussex*, p. 10.
5. Pamela Horn, *Life Below Stairs in the 20th Century*, p. 43.
6. Ibid., p. 49.
7. Ibid., p. 43.
8. Ibid., p. 175.
9. Ibid., p. 180.
10. The debacle is related by Frances Spalding in her excellent biography, *Vanessa Bell*, p. 178.
11. Angelica's conception was a result of what may have been the only night Duncan and Vanessa ever spent together. For respectability's sake she was brought up as the daughter of Clive Bell. Grace never commented – even in her private diaries – on whether or not she suspected this fact; no doubt she quietly worked it out as the years passed.
12. This is confirmed in a letter from Vanessa to Angelica written on 12 May 1945: 'Do you know that Grace will have been with us 25 years on May 30th? What are we to do about it?' From Regina Marler, ed., *Selected Letters of Vanessa Bell*, p. 498.
13. Diana Higgens, *Grace at Charleston: Memories and Recipes*.
14. Frances Spalding, *Duncan Grant*, p. 258.

TWO

1. Louie Dunnett replaced Grace as nanny to the Bell children when Grace became housemaid.
2. Interview in the *Brighton Evening Argus*, 6 February 1981.
3. Originally Lopoukhova and slightly anglicised by Lydia to Lopokova.
4. Spalding, *Duncan Grant*, p. 258.
5. The Bell family's 'daily' Mrs Uppington.
6. Spalding, *Duncan Grant*, p.287.

THREE

1. Vanessa's friend and former lover, the artist and critic Roger Fry (1866–1934) who, though not staying at La Maison Blanche, was also spending the winter in St Tropez.
2. Dorothy Strachey Bussy (1865–1960), sister of Lytton Strachey (1880–1932), wife of the French painter Simon Bussy (1870–1954) and lover of Lady Ottoline Morrell (1873–1938).
3. Rose Vildrac was the wife of the French poet and gallery owner Charles Vildrac (1882–1971).
4. The Polish-British painter and critic Romuald 'Rom' Landau (1899–1974).

Notes and References

5. Vanessa writing to Virginia from Villa Corsica, Cassis on 22 February 1927 (Marler, ed., *Selected Letters*, p. 308).
6. Tate Archive, London: Charleston Correspondence, TGA 8010.

FOUR

1. Spalding, *Vanessa Bell*, p. 181.
2. Spalding, *Duncan Grant*, p. 258.
3. Ibid., p. 258.
4. Ibid., p. 325.
5. Ibid., p. 258.

FIVE

1. 22 February 1927, Marler, ed., *Selected Letters*, p. 308.
2. Spalding, *Duncan Grant*, p. 299.

SIX

1. Interview in the *Brighton Evening Argus*, 6 February 1981.
2. Ibid.
3. British Library, London: Higgens Papers, vol. i (Add MS 83198).
4. 10 October 1936, *Selected Letters of Vanessa Bell*, p. 425.
5. British Library, London: Higgens Papers, vol. i (Add MS 83198).
6. Ibid.
7. Ibid.
8. British Library, London: Higgens Papers, vol. iii (ff. 81) (Add MS 83200).
9. British Library, London: Higgens Papers, vol. i (Add MS 83198).
10. Ibid.
11. Ibid.
12. Jane 'Janie' Bussy (1906–1960), daughter of Duncan's cousin Dorothy Strachey and the French painter Simon Bussy.
13. 6 June 1940, Marler, ed., *Selected Letters*, p. 468.
14. In the seven-year period (1897–1904) between the deaths of Vanessa's stepsister Stella Duckworth Hill and father Sir Leslie Stephen.
15. It was said that Logan Thompson and Lydia Lopokova enjoyed a torrid affair.
16. Lottie Hope was initially maid to Virginia Woolf and then Clive Bell's cook in London, before, in 1935 (upon the birth of John Higgens), coming to Charleston as cook under Grace as housekeeper.
17. To Jane Bussy, 13 January 1941, Marler, ed., *Selected Letters*, p. 472.
18. 18 May 1945, Marler, ed., *Selected Letters*, p. 497.

19. 1 December 1952, Marler, ed., *Selected Letters*, p. 536.
20. BBC radio serial drama running from 1948 to 1969 concerning the middle-class doctor's wife Mrs Dale and her family. According to Henrietta Garnett, Vanessa and Duncan loathed *The Archers*.
21. Spalding, *Vanessa Bell*, p. 307.
22. 7 February 1930, Marler, ed., *Selected Letters*, p. 351.
23. 20 January 1960, ibid., p. 547.
24. 24 January 1960, ibid., pp. 549–50.

SEVEN

1. Without any form of religious service, Vanessa's burial proved a very quiet affair and she was interred discreetly at Firle churchyard.
2. Quentin described Grace as 'the guardian angel of Charleston' in *Bloomsbury Recalled*, p. 91. The epithet was probably coined by Duncan.
3. Julia Prinsep, Lady Stephen (1846–1895); an inspiration for Mrs Ramsey in Virginia Woolf's *To the Lighthouse* (1927).
4. Spalding, *Duncan Grant*, p. 435.
5. Ibid., p. 465.
6. Ibid., p. 471.
7. Interview in the *Brighton Evening Argus*, 6 February 1981.
8. Spalding, *Duncan Grant*, p. 479.
9. Interview in the *Brighton Evening Argus*, 6 February 1981.
10. Ibid., 6 February 1981.

Bibliography

Quentin Bell, *Bloomsbury Recalled* (New York: Columbia University Press, 1995)
Quentin Bell and Virginia Nicholson, *Charleston: A Bloomsbury House and Garden* (London: Frances Lincoln, 1997)
Vanessa Bell, *Sketches in Pen and Ink: A Bloomsbury Notebook*, ed. Lia Giachero (London: Hogarth, 2007)
E. M. Forster, *Howards End* (1910; Harmondsworth: Penguin, 1989)
E. M. Forster, *A Passage to India* (1924; London: Penguin, 2005)
Angelica Garnett, *Deceived with Kindness: A Bloomsbury Childhood* (London: Chatto & Windus, 1984)
Victoria Glendinning, *Vita: The Life of Vita Sackville-West* (London: Penguin, 1983)
Alexandra Harris, *Romantic Moderns: English Writers, Artists and the Imagination* (London: Thames & Hudson, 2010)

Notes and References

Diana Higgens, *Grace at Charleston: Memories and Recipes* (private publication)
Pamela Horn, *Life Below Stairs in the 20th Century* (Stroud: Sutton, 2003)
Pamela Horn, *The Rise and Fall of the Victorian Servant* (Stroud: Sutton, 1997)
Hermione Lee, *Virginia Woolf* (London: Vintage, 2007)
Paul Levy, *Moore: G. E. Moore and the Cambridge Apostles* (London: Weidenfeld & Nicolson, 1979)
Alison Light, *Mrs Woolf and the Servants* (London: Fig Tree, 2007)
Regina Marler, ed., *Selected Letters of Vanessa Bell* (London: Bloomsbury, 1994)
Richard Overy, *The Morbid Age: Britain Between the Wars* (London: Allen Lane, 2009)
S. P. Rosenbaum, ed., *The Bloomsbury Group: A Collection of Memories, Commentary and Criticism* (London: Croom Helm, 1975)
Frances Spalding, *Duncan Grant* (London: Chatto & Windus, 1997)
Frances Spalding, *Vanessa Bell* (1983; Stroud: Tempus, 2006)
Simon Watney, *Bloomsbury in Sussex* (Lewes: Snake River Press, 2007)
Virginia Woolf, *Between the Acts* (1941; Cambridge: Cambridge University Press, 2011)
Virginia Woolf, *Mr Bennett and Mrs Brown* (London: Hogarth Press, 1924).
Virginia Woolf, *To the Lighthouse* (London: Hogarth Press, 1927).

Image Credits

Index

Figures in *italic* refer to pages on which illustrations appear.

Alciston, East Sussex 86
Alfriston, East Sussex 124
Alice (housemaid) 79, 83, 84, 93, 94, 103, 106
Anghilanti, Elise *63*
Annan, Noel 17
Annie (cook) 52, 94
Arts and Crafts Movement 16
Ashcroft, Peggy 132
Ashton, Sir Frederick 132
Attlee, Clement 96

Bagenal, Barbara *47*, 131
Bagenal, Judith *47*, 83, 105
Banham, Norfolk 17, 132
Barley Mow pub, Selmeston, East Sussex 81, 82, 86, 105–6, 124
Becker, Walter 74
Beddington, Sussex, Asheham House 14
Bell, Angelica (later Garnett) *8*, *47*, *69*, *90*, *100*; as daughter of Duncan Grant 22, 136; relationship with Grace 28, 122; in traffic accident 31; in France 39, 43–6, 49, 55, 59–60, 66; tutored in French 66; away at school 70; in London 83; Vanessa on 99; at Charleston 105; letters from Vanessa 119–20, 121; and Vanessa's death 130

Bell, Anne Olivier (wife of Quentin) 6
Bell, Clive *13*, 26–7, *38*; relationship with Vanessa 11, 39; relationship with Grace 31, 93; flirtation with Grace 70, 79; as financial adviser to Grace 106; letter from Walter Higgens 111; provides game at Charleston 117
Bell, Cressida 19, 20, 121, 122, 126, 142
Bell, Julian (son of Clive and Vanessa) 22, 31, *38*, 86, *100*; on Grace 35; in France 39, 43–50, 53, 56–80, 75; at Cambridge 70; at Charleston 79, 81, 104–5, 108; death in Spanish Civil War 99, 131
Bell, Julian (son of Quentin) 129–30
Bell, Quentin 22, 31, 86, 92, *100*, 135, 142; memories of Grace 23; in London 28; interview with Grace 36, 131–2; in France 39, 43–50, 55, 58–60, 75, 81; letter to Duncan Grant 66–70; at Leighton Park School, Reading 70; at Charleston 104–5, 108; makes effigy of Hitler 119; and Vanessa's death 129–30
Bell, Vanessa *8*, *10*; character and personality 11–14, 39; relationship with Duncan Grant 11, 102; at Charleston 16, 27; in Bloomsbury 26–7; paintings 30; *The Kitchen* 36, 106, *107*; in France

Index

39, 43, 44, 48–50, 52, 54, 57, 59, 61, 62,
75; on Grace's beauty 79–81; letter to
Virginia about Grace 98–9; and
Julian's death 99; correspondence with
Grace 113–16; in Second World War
116; as householder 117; *Annunciation*
118; *Nativity* 118; on VE Day 120; as
driver 125; letter to Jane Bussy about
Grace 125–6; illness and death 129–30,
141–2; *see also* Higgens, Grace,
relationship with Vanessa
Blanche (parlour-maid) 52
Bloomsbury Group: ubiquity 3–4;
philosophy of 11–14
Bouvet, Mademoiselle 45, 64
Boxall, Nellie 31, 35
British Library, Grace Higgens Archive 5,
6–7, 134
Brittain, Nellie 39, 43, 44, 46, 48, 49, 50,
52–62, 74, 76
Bussy, Dorothy 59, 125
Bussy, Jane 116, 125–6
Bussy family 129

Cambridge, University of 70
Cameron, Julia Margaret 36
Campbell, Jean 66
Cassis, France 35, 44, 66–70, *68*, 73–4; La
Bergère 66, *67*, 70, 115; Villa Corsica
66
Charleston Farmhouse, near Lewes, East
Sussex *2*, 16–17, 27, 36, 45, 70, 86,
102–26, 131–7, 141–4, *143*;
improvements to 120, 125; garden *140*;
kitchen 36, 105, 108, 117–19, 121, 126,
130, 144
Charlie (army chef) 120
Chevalier, Madame 66, *69*
Churchill, Winston 91
Colefax, Lady Sybil 79
Coles, Ruby 84, 106, 120
Collins agency, Norwich 20
Czechoslovakia 114

Daily Express 20
Dufferin and Ava, Sheridan, Marquess of
81
Dunnett, Louie 31, 79–81, 83, 84, 93, 94,
102, 105, 106

Eastbourne, Sussex 106
Eliot, T. S. 131
Elizabeth II, Queen 81; Coronation 120
Emily (housemaid) 94
Enlightenment 11

Firle, Sussex 14; Little Talland House 14;
Beacon 105; Village Shop 117, *133*
Firle Park, Sussex 16
First World War 20, 21, 86, 98, 115
Ford, Albert 102–3
Forster, E. M. ('Morgan') 126, 132;
Howards End 14, 16; *Where Angels Fear
to Tread* 62
Fothergill, Mrs 58
France 39–70, 111, 129, 132; *see also*
Cassis; St Tropez
Freud, Sigmund, *The Interpretation of
Dreams* 31–2
Fry, Roger 40, *41*, 43, 44, 48, 50, 51, 59,
64, 103, 131

Gage, Lord 16
Garnett, Angelica *see* Bell, Angelica
Garnett, David 'Bunny' 16, 23, 121
Garnett, Henrietta 7, 23, 74, 121–2, 135,
137, 142
Garnett, Nerissa 125
George V, King 29
Germany, Alice (Grace's sister) 29–30,
118
Germany, Elizabeth (Grace's mother) 17,
19–20, 22, 50, 58, 60, 82
Germany, George (Grace's father) 17, 50
Gogol, Nikolai 32; *Dead Souls* 31
Grant, Duncan *12*, 62, *128*; admiration of
Grace 5, 32, 78–9, 87; calls Grace
'angel of Charleston' 5; friendship with
Grace 6, 108, 124, 130–1, 135–6, 141–2;
character and personality 11, 14; at
Charleston 16, 102–3, 108; and
Angelica 22, 136; in Bloomsbury 26;
portrait of Grace 36; in France 39, 43,
44, 48–50, 58–60, 62; illness in Cassis
66; Valentine's card sent to Grace 79,
80; wedding present to Grace and
Walter 86; and birth of Grace's son
John 111, 113; in Second World War
116; as driver 124–5; and Vanessa's

death 130; death 142
Grant, Ethel (Duncan's mother) 113
Grigorescu, Lucian 73–4
Guinness, Lindy 81

Hampshire Cyclists 86
Harland, Mr 94, 98
Harland, Mrs 79, 82, 93, 96–7, 98, 106
Hayes, Middlesex 19, 23
Hazel, Mrs 58
Heath, Edward 125
Hecks, Mr 16
Higgens, Diana (Grace's daughter-in-law)
  21, 86, 120, 124; *Grace at Charleston* 23
Higgens, Grace (née Germany) *18*, *63*, *69*,
  72, *76*, *85*, *90*, *112*, *133*, *134*, *140*, *143*;
  called 'angel of Charleston' 5, 130;
  relationship with Duncan Grant 5, 6,
  32, 78–9, 87, 108, 124, 130–1, 135–6,
  141–2; relationship with Vanessa Bell 5,
  6, 31, 36, 66, 92, 93, 98–9, 104, 109,
  111, 113–16, 117, 124, 135–7, 141; years
  in service 5; early years 17–19; diaries
  19, 22, 24, 28, 34–5, 73–4, 91, 93, 94–5,
  137–8; hired by Vanessa Bell to work at
  Charleston 22–4; in London 28–9;
  enjoyment of reading 31–2, 119; in
  Gordon Square kitchen 32, 81, 83, 94;
  voice and accent 35–6; in Charleston
  kitchen 36, 105, 108, 117–19, 121, 126,
  130, 144; interviewed by Quentin Bell
  36, 131–2; portrait by Duncan Grant
  36; sits for Vanessa Bell and Duncan
  Grant 36; in St Tropez kitchen 43, 60,
  61; as swimmer 43, 44, 49; learns
  French 44, 66; 'Things I Noticed in St
  Tropez' 64–6; in Cassis 66–70, 73–4;
  good looks and stylishness 73, 76–82,
  87, 97; and Grigorescu 74; romantic
  interests 74–6; rejected admirers 81–6;
  as housekeeper at Charleston 86,
  109–11, 117–18; marries Walter
  Higgens 86, 109–11; period of boredom
  and depression 91–2; political views
  95–6, 108, 125; feminism and views on
  men 97; character and personality 99,
  121–2, 125–6, 136, 144; at Charleston
  102–26; and stock market 106;
  pregnancy and birth of John 111–13;

secretarial duties 111, 130; as gardener
  117–18; love of animals 118; injury to
  spine 121; relationship with young
  children 121–2; exhaustion and tears
  125; and prisoners of war 126; and issue
  of retirement 131; retirement aged 68
  132
Higgens, John (Grace's son) 5, 19, 20, 29,
  39, 74, 86, 106, 108–9, *112*, 113, 117,
  118, 120, *123*, 124, 137, 138; poses for
  Vanessa 118
Higgens, Walter (Grace's husband) 86,
  108–11, 119, *123*, 124, 131, 132, *133*, 141;
  called by Vanessa 'the Dolt' 108, 116,
  119–20, 121; letter to Clive Bell 111;
  Henrietta Garnett on 122
Hitler, Adolf 115, 119
Hogarth Press 32
Hope, Lottie 35, 93, 119
Horn, Pamela 21
Hugo, Victor 60
Huxley, Julian 131

International Brigade 99
Italy 111, 113

Kemp (soldier) 103
Keynes, John Maynard 6, 32, *33*, 34, 84,
  86, 118

Landau, Romuald 'Rom' 61, 64, 69, 74,
  75–6
Lawrence, D. H., *Lady Chatterley's Lover*
  32
Leighton Park School, Reading 70
Lloyd, Marie 132
London: Gordon Square 22, 32, 45, 81,
  102, 132; Bloomsbury (district) 26–7;
  British Museum 26; Slade School of Art
  26; University College 26; Tottenham
  Court Road 29, 30, 92; C & A 78;
  Kingsway Theatre 83; Lyons teahouse,
  Oxford Street 83; department stores 95;
  Hampstead Road 95; Old Compton
  Street 95; Fitzroy Street 109; Tavistock
  Square 109
Lopokova, Lydia ('Loppy') 6, 32–4, *33*,
  84, 118
Louise (French daily) 43–4, 46, 59, 60, 61

Index

Manners, Lady Diana 79
Margaret, Princess 81
Mary (housemaid) 22
Mayer, Louie 35
Medley, Robert 32
Menton 129
Mills, Sheldon 17
Moore, G. E., *Principia Ethica* 11
Morier, J. J. *Hajji Baba* 31
Morris, William 16
Mrs Dale's Diary 121
Munich 70
Munich Agreement 115

Neil, Captain 83
New House Farm, East Sussex 16
Norfolk 22, 95, 118
Norwich 20, 21

Otto, Madame 126

Paris 64
Partridge, Sophie (daughter of Henrietta
    Garnett) 122
Patmore, Coventry, 'The Angel in the
    House' 130
Paul (farm hand?) 106
Pears, Peter 132
Pelling, Lionel 106
Perugia 113
Priestley, J. B., *The Good Companions* 79

Ringmer, East Sussex 132, 142
Roche, Clarissa 135
Roche, Paul 135
Rodmell, Sussex, Monk's House 16, 109,
    113
Romanian Academy 74
Romantic movement 11
Rome 111, 113
Roquebrune, La Souco 129

Sackville-West, Vita 3
St Petersburg, Alexandrinsky Theatre 32
St Raphael, France 40
St Tropez, France 39, 40–66, 75, 91, 93;

La Maison Blanche 42–3; L'Hotel Zube
    58; Cathedral 65
Santucci, Madame 60, 61, 62
Santucci, Monsieur 60, 64
Second World War 27, 96, 115–16; Victory
    Week 119–20
Shone, Richard 23, 31–2, 34, 74, 78, 116,
    125, 142
Sickert, Walter 132
Sitwell, Osbert 131
Spalding, Frances 17, 23, 32, 79, 122, 132
Spanish Civil War 99
Sprott, Sebastian 86
Sprowart, Dr 20
Stephen, Adrian 103–4
Stephen, Karin (Adrian's wife) 103–4
Strachey, James 32
Strachey, Lytton 32, 103
Swift, Jonathan, *Gulliver's Travels* 31

Teed, Colonel 66
Thompson, Logan 117–18
Tilton, Sussex 34, 84, 118, 119
The Times 21

Uppington, Mrs 35, 83, 94, 102, 106

Vence, France 59
Vildrac, Charles 64
Vildrac, Rose 60, 61–2, 64

Watney, Simon 17
Weller, Edgar 81–2, 83–4, 106, 120
Weller family 119
West, Arthur (gardener) 102–3, 106
West, Tom 83, 103
West family 119
White, Charlie 103, 106
Woolf, Leonard *15*, 16, 104, 117
Woolf, Virginia (née Stephen) 5, 14, *15*,
    30, 66; at Asheham 16; novels 30, 31;
    and servants 31, 35, 36; Vanessa's letter
    to 98–9; Grace on 103–4; notes to
    Grace 109, *110*, 113, *114*

Zube, Madame 58

153

The Charleston Bulletin Supplements
Virginia Woolf & Quentin Bell
Edited by Claudia Olk

In the summer of 1923 Virginia Woolf's nephews, Quentin and Julian Bell, founded a family newspaper, *The Charleston Bulletin*. Quentin decided to ask his aunt Virginia for a contribution: 'it seemed stupid to have a real author so close at hand and not have her contribute'. They joined forces, and from 1923 until 1927 created fully fledged booklets of stories and drawings that were announced as Supplements. Written or dictated by Woolf and illustrated by Quentin, these Supplements present a unique collaboration between the novelist during her most prolific years and the child-painter. In Virginia Woolf, Quentin Bell found not only a professional author and an experienced journalist, but, above all, a close companion and conspirator who shared his irreverence and mischievous sense of humour.

ISBN 978 0 7123 5891 0   £12.99

The Spoken Word
The Bloomsbury Group

The Bloomsbury Group remains of great public interest for its influence on art, literature and politics in the first half of the twentieth century. Recordings of this informal association of writers, artists and intellectuals are brought together for the first time on a 2CD set. The recordings also include reminiscences by some of those who were associated or related to the group. The CDs draw on long-unheard BBC broadcasts and recordings from the Charleston Trust, most of which are published for the first time.

ISBN 978 0 7123 0593 8   Two CDs £16.00